Developing Cross-Platform Apps with Flutter: A Practical Approach

A Step-by-Step Guide to Building Mobile Apps with Flutter

BOOZMAN RICHARD

BOOKER BLUNT

Table of Content

TABLE OF CONTENTS

INTRODUCTION

Developing Cross-Platform Apps with Flutter: A Practical Approach

Mobile app development has witnessed an incredible transformation in recent years. As businesses and developers strive to reach wider audiences across multiple platforms, the need for cross-platform development solutions has grown significantly. Among the most powerful and efficient tools for creating high-quality, high-performance apps for iOS, Android, and beyond, **Flutter** has emerged as a leading framework.

This book, **"Developing Cross-Platform Apps with Flutter: A Practical Approach,"** is designed to equip you with the skills and knowledge necessary to leverage Flutter in building apps that perform seamlessly across multiple platforms, using a single codebase. Whether you are a beginner just starting your journey into mobile app development, or an experienced developer looking to expand your expertise with Flutter, this book offers a comprehensive and hands-on guide to building beautiful, high-performance applications.

What is Flutter?

Flutter, developed by Google, is an open-source framework that allows developers to build natively compiled applications for mobile, web, and desktop from a single codebase. Unlike traditional cross-platform frameworks that use a JavaScript bridge, Flutter uses **Dart**, a language also created by Google, which compiles directly to native code. This results in faster performance and a more seamless user experience. One of the most appealing features of Flutter is its highly customizable and expressive UI toolkit, which allows developers to create stunning, responsive, and smooth user interfaces.

Why Flutter for Cross-Platform Development?

In the world of mobile app development, there are a variety of options for building apps across multiple platforms. Native development for each platform—iOS and Android—can be costly, time-consuming, and requires knowledge of two different programming languages and toolsets. Cross-platform frameworks like React Native, Xamarin, and Ionic have tried to solve this problem, but Flutter stands out due to its:

1. **Native Performance**: Flutter uses a custom rendering engine that ensures apps built with it have near-native performance.

7

2. **Single Codebase**: Instead of maintaining separate codebases for iOS and Android, you only need to write your code once, saving both time and resources.

3. **Fast Development Cycle**: Flutter's **hot reload** feature allows you to make changes to the code and immediately see those changes reflected in the app, significantly speeding up development.

4. **Rich Ecosystem**: With an ever-growing set of plugins and tools, Flutter supports everything from network requests to local storage to camera and GPS functionalities, making it a powerful toolkit for any developer.

What Will You Learn in This Book?

This book takes a practical, hands-on approach to teaching you Flutter development. It starts from the very basics, helping you get set up and build your first app, and gradually moves to more advanced topics. Each chapter is designed to build on the previous one, providing you with a structured learning path.

Here's a sneak peek at what you'll learn:

1. **Introduction to Flutter and Cross-Platform Development**: You'll start by understanding the

fundamentals of mobile app development and why cross-platform frameworks like Flutter are gaining popularity.

2. **Setting Up Your Development Environment**: Learn how to install Flutter, set up Android Studio and Visual Studio Code, and create your first Flutter app.

3. **Understanding Dart and Flutter Architecture**: Since Flutter is based on the Dart programming language, you'll dive into Dart's core concepts and learn about Flutter's widget-based architecture.

4. **Building Responsive UIs**: Learn how to design beautiful user interfaces that work seamlessly on both iOS and Android with Flutter's wide range of customizable widgets.

5. **State Management and Navigation**: Explore how to manage app state and handle navigation between different screens, a crucial part of any mobile app.

6. **Working with APIs and Local Storage**: Learn how to fetch data from APIs and store it locally on the device, enabling you to build dynamic apps that communicate with the outside world.

7. **Adding Animations and Customization**: Understand how to create stunning animations and customize the UI to match your app's branding.

8. **Testing, Debugging, and Optimization**: Learn how to write unit tests, debug your app, and optimize its performance for a smooth user experience.

9. **Building and Deploying Your App**: The final chapters guide you through the process of building your app for release, including signing and uploading it to the Google Play Store and Apple App Store.

Who is This Book For?

This book is for:

- **Beginner Developers**: If you're new to mobile development, this book will introduce you to the world of Flutter and guide you through building your first app step-by-step.
- **Experienced Developers**: If you're already familiar with programming, especially with other mobile frameworks like React Native or Xamarin, this book will help you quickly grasp Flutter's unique features and advantages.
- **Cross-Platform Enthusiasts**: If you're interested in building apps that work seamlessly across multiple platforms, this book will show you how Flutter can be the solution you've been looking for.

Comprehensive and Practical: Each chapter is packed with detailed explanations and real-world examples. You will not only learn how to use Flutter's features, but also how to implement them in real-world scenarios.

Step-by-Step Instructions: The book follows a structured approach, starting with the basics and gradually building up to more advanced topics. With clear explanations and practical code examples, you'll be able to follow along and apply what you learn immediately.

Focus on Performance: Flutter is known for its high performance. This book emphasizes building apps that are optimized for speed, responsiveness, and smooth UI rendering.

A Real-World Approach: Throughout the book, you will build several fully-functional apps, which will help you understand the core concepts and best practices of Flutter development.

By the end of this book, you will have a solid understanding of how to build cross-platform apps with Flutter. You will be able to create beautiful, high-performance apps for both iOS and Android, with the flexibility to extend them to the web and desktop in the future. Flutter's growing ecosystem and powerful features make it an exciting tool for developers, and this book aims to equip you with everything you need to get started and succeed in the world of mobile development.

Whether you're a complete beginner or an experienced developer, this book will provide you with the knowledge and skills to create top-notch cross-platform applications with Flutter.

Ready to start your journey with Flutter? Let's dive into the world of mobile app development and unlock the power of Flutter!

CHAPTER 1

INTRODUCTION TO MOBILE APP DEVELOPMENT

Overview of Mobile App Development

Mobile app development is the process of creating software applications that run on mobile devices, such as smartphones and tablets. These apps can be built for various platforms, such as Android, iOS, or Windows, and can range from simple utilities to complex, feature-rich applications used in daily life. With the growing reliance on smartphones, mobile apps have become essential for businesses, entertainment, communication, and education.

Mobile apps are typically categorized into three types:

1. **Native Apps**: Developed for a specific platform (Android or iOS) using the platform's native programming language (Java or Kotlin for Android, Swift or Objective-C for iOS).
2. **Web Apps**: Accessed through a web browser, web apps are essentially websites optimized for mobile devices.

3. **Hybrid/Cross-Platform Apps**: These apps are designed to run on multiple platforms with a single codebase, minimizing development time and cost.

The mobile app development process involves several stages, including planning, design, development, testing, and deployment. The choice of development approach—whether native or cross-platform—affects many aspects of the app's development, including performance, user experience, and long-term maintainability.

Differences Between Native and Cross-Platform Development

The choice between native and cross-platform development depends on various factors like budget, timeline, app functionality, and target audience. Here's a breakdown of the key differences:

1. **Native Development**:
   - **Platform-Specific**: Native apps are written in the programming languages specific to each platform (e.g., Java/Kotlin for Android, Swift for iOS).
   - **Performance**: Native apps tend to offer superior performance because they directly utilize the device's hardware and software.

14

- o **User Experience**: Native apps can fully leverage the platform's design guidelines and native components, providing a seamless user experience tailored to that operating system.
- o **Maintenance**: Native development requires separate codebases for each platform, making updates and bug fixes more time-consuming and costly.

2. **Cross-Platform Development**:

- o **Single Codebase**: Cross-platform development allows developers to write one codebase that runs on multiple platforms (Android, iOS, etc.), saving time and effort.
- o **Performance**: While cross-platform apps are generally slower than native apps due to the additional layer of abstraction, frameworks like Flutter have narrowed this gap by offering near-native performance.
- o **User Experience**: Cross-platform apps can offer a similar user experience across platforms, but there may be limitations in accessing platform-specific UI components and functionality.
- o **Maintenance**: Cross-platform apps are easier to maintain since developers only need to update one codebase. This can be a major advantage in terms of cost-effectiveness and time efficiency.

The Benefits and Challenges of Cross-Platform Apps

Benefits:

1. **Cost Efficiency**: Since you can use a single codebase for both Android and iOS, cross-platform development saves significant costs related to hiring separate developers for each platform.

2. **Faster Development**: Developing a single app for multiple platforms speeds up the overall development cycle, allowing businesses to launch their apps quicker and reach a broader audience.

3. **Code Reusability**: Cross-platform development frameworks allow the reuse of most of the code across platforms, which reduces development time and simplifies updates.

4. **Consistency Across Platforms**: Cross-platform development ensures a consistent user interface and experience across Android and iOS, which can be crucial for brand identity.

5. **Access to Native Features**: Modern cross-platform frameworks like Flutter provide access to native features (camera, GPS, sensors, etc.) without the need to write platform-specific code.

Challenges:

1. **Performance Issues**: Although frameworks like Flutter offer near-native performance, cross-platform apps may still have performance bottlenecks in certain scenarios, especially for complex animations and graphics.

2. **Limited Access to Platform-Specific APIs**: While most cross-platform frameworks provide access to common APIs, certain advanced or platform-specific features may be difficult or impossible to implement. This can require writing custom native code.

3. **User Interface Consistency**: Ensuring that the user interface looks and behaves consistently across platforms can be a challenge, especially when the two platforms have different design guidelines (Material Design for Android vs. Human Interface Guidelines for iOS).

4. **Dependency on Framework Updates**: Cross-platform frameworks rely on third-party developers for updates and bug fixes. If the framework is slow to support new platform versions or features, developers may face delays in implementing those features.

5. **Learning Curve**: Although Flutter simplifies cross-platform development, developers who are familiar with native languages may face a learning curve when transitioning to a framework like Flutter.

Conclusion

Cross-platform development offers significant advantages in terms of speed, cost, and simplicity by allowing developers to use a single codebase across multiple platforms. However, there are also challenges, particularly when it comes to performance, user interface consistency, and accessing platform-specific features. Flutter stands out as a powerful framework for cross-platform development, bridging the gap between native performance and cross-platform convenience.

As we dive deeper into the world of Flutter, you'll learn how to leverage this framework's full potential to build robust, efficient, and attractive mobile apps for both Android and iOS.

CHAPTER 2

WHY FLUTTER?

Introduction to Flutter

Flutter is an open-source UI toolkit developed by Google for building natively compiled applications for mobile, web, and desktop from a single codebase. It was first introduced in 2017 and has since gained significant popularity among developers due to its flexibility, performance, and ease of use. Unlike other cross-platform frameworks that rely on web views or native code bridges, Flutter uses its own rendering engine to produce high-performance applications that feel and behave like native apps.

At its core, Flutter uses **Dart**, a programming language created by Google, to write the app's code. Dart is easy to learn for developers familiar with languages like JavaScript or Java, and it provides features such as asynchronous programming and strong type-checking to make development smoother.

Flutter allows developers to create a wide range of apps, including mobile applications for both Android and iOS, web apps, and even desktop applications for macOS, Linux, and Windows. The toolkit includes rich pre-designed widgets, a fast development cycle with hot reload, and built-in tools for testing and debugging, making it an ideal choice for many developers seeking to streamline their app development process.

Flutter vs. Other Cross-Platform Frameworks (e.g., React Native, Xamarin)

To understand why Flutter is often the preferred choice for cross-platform app development, it's essential to compare it to other popular cross-platform frameworks like **React Native** and **Xamarin**. Here's how Flutter stacks up against these frameworks:

1. **Flutter vs. React Native**:
    o   **Language**: React Native uses **JavaScript**, one of the most popular programming languages, whereas Flutter uses **Dart**. For JavaScript developers, React Native may seem like the easier option due to their familiarity with the language. However, Dart's syntax is similar to other object-oriented languages (such as Java or C#), which may be appealing to developers from different backgrounds.
    o   **Performance**: React Native uses **bridging** to communicate with native code, which can sometimes result in performance bottlenecks, especially for complex animations and resource-heavy applications. In contrast, Flutter does not

rely on bridges and uses a **skia engine** to render UI elements directly. This results in smoother animations and higher performance overall.

- o **Development Speed**: Both frameworks support **hot reload**, which allows developers to see changes instantly during development. However, Flutter's "widget-based" architecture, where everything is a widget (including layout elements), provides a more streamlined and flexible way to design UI, reducing the need for customization compared to React Native's native components.

- o **UI Customization**: Flutter provides a **highly customizable UI** with pre-built widgets that match both iOS and Android design languages (Material Design and Cupertino). React Native, while offering a native look and feel, may require additional work to customize UI elements to match each platform's specific design guidelines.

2. **Flutter vs. Xamarin**:

- o **Language**: Xamarin uses **C#** and the .NET framework for app development, which is suitable for developers who are already familiar with C# or .NET technologies. On the other hand, Flutter uses Dart, which may be unfamiliar to most developers but is easy to learn for those with a background in other modern programming languages.

o **Performance**: Xamarin apps are compiled into native code, but it still relies on a lot of .NET bindings to interact with platform-specific APIs. This adds a layer of abstraction that can reduce performance. Flutter, by contrast, compiles directly to native code, offering faster startup times and better performance, especially for graphics-intensive applications.

o **Community and Ecosystem**: While Xamarin is backed by Microsoft and has a strong developer base, Flutter's ecosystem has grown rapidly, with an active community and many third-party libraries available to simplify development. Flutter's ecosystem is especially vibrant in mobile development, while Xamarin also offers a good set of tools for building cross-platform apps for mobile, desktop, and even wearables.

o **App Size**: Xamarin apps tend to have a larger binary size due to the overhead introduced by the .NET runtime. Flutter apps, however, may also have larger binaries than some native apps, but Flutter's ability to compile to native code generally results in smaller app sizes than those built with Xamarin.

Advantages of Using Flutter for App Development

Flutter has become the go-to choice for many developers for a variety of reasons. Let's explore the key advantages that make Flutter stand out in the realm of cross-platform mobile app development:

1. **Single Codebase for Multiple Platforms**: One of the biggest advantages of Flutter is its ability to write a **single codebase** that runs on multiple platforms, including Android, iOS, and even web and desktop apps. This eliminates the need for separate development teams for each platform and saves time and money in the development process.

2. **High Performance**: Flutter's performance is one of its strongest selling points. Unlike other cross-platform frameworks that rely on a bridge between the app and native code, Flutter's **direct compilation** to native code (ARM code for mobile apps) ensures fast startup times and smooth animations, delivering near-native performance without the overhead of a JavaScript bridge or other intermediary layers.

3. **Rich UI Customization**: Flutter provides a wide range of **pre-built widgets** that are customizable to suit both **Android and iOS design guidelines**. The **Material Design** widgets for Android and **Cupertino** widgets for

iOS make it easy to create visually consistent and beautiful apps without worrying about adapting to different platform styles.

4. **Hot Reload**: Flutter's **hot reload** feature allows developers to instantly see changes in the app without restarting it, making the development process faster and more efficient. This is particularly useful for tweaking the UI and iterating on the app's design.

5. **Growing Ecosystem and Community**: Since its release, Flutter has seen an enormous growth in its community and ecosystem. Developers have access to a growing number of third-party packages and libraries that simplify tasks like state management, networking, and database access. The active Flutter community provides plenty of support, resources, and tutorials, helping developers overcome any obstacles they encounter.

6. **Strong Documentation and Resources**: Flutter comes with comprehensive **documentation** that makes it easy for developers to get started. The official Flutter website, as well as community-driven resources, provide detailed examples, best practices, and troubleshooting tips, ensuring a smooth learning curve.

7. **Open Source**: Flutter is open-source, meaning that developers have the freedom to contribute to the framework and improve it. The open-source nature also

makes it free to use, which is particularly appealing to startups and individual developers.

8. **Support for Integration**: Flutter provides strong support for integrating with **native code**, enabling developers to include features that require platform-specific functionality (e.g., accessing device sensors, using camera APIs, or implementing platform-specific UI elements). Flutter allows you to access native Android and iOS APIs using **platform channels**, providing flexibility without sacrificing performance.

9. **Growing Adoption by Large Companies**: Many well-known companies are adopting Flutter for their app development. Companies like Google (with Google Ads), Alibaba, eBay, and BMW have built successful apps using Flutter. This growth in adoption is a testament to the framework's stability and capability to build scalable and reliable apps.

Conclusion

Flutter is rapidly becoming the preferred choice for many developers who want to create high-performance, cross-platform apps with a single codebase. With its robust set of tools, strong community support, and impressive performance capabilities, Flutter provides a compelling solution for app development across mobile, web, and desktop platforms.

By choosing Flutter, developers can enjoy the best of both worlds: the speed and efficiency of cross-platform development combined with the performance and native feel typically associated with platform-specific apps. As you progress in your Flutter journey, you'll see how it provides the tools necessary to build beautiful, scalable, and performant applications.

CHAPTER 3

SETTING UP YOUR DEVELOPMENT ENVIRONMENT

Installing Flutter SDK on Windows, macOS, and Linux

To begin developing with Flutter, the first step is to set up the Flutter SDK (Software Development Kit) on your machine. The installation process differs slightly depending on your operating system. Here are the steps for each platform:

1. Installing Flutter on Windows

1. **Download Flutter SDK**:
   - o Go to the official Flutter website at flutter.dev and navigate to the "Get Started" section.
   - o Under the "Windows" tab, download the stable Flutter SDK zip file.
2. **Extract the Flutter SDK**:
   - o After downloading the Flutter SDK, extract the contents to an appropriate location on your computer (e.g., `C:\src\flutter`).

27

- o Avoid extracting the Flutter SDK to a path that contains spaces (e.g., `C:\Program Files\`), as it may cause issues with Flutter tools.

3. **Update Your Path**:

- o Add the Flutter tool to your system's PATH. Right-click on "This PC" or "Computer" and select "Properties." Click on "Advanced system settings" and then "Environment Variables."

- o In the "System variables" section, select "Path" and click "Edit." Add the full path to the `flutter\bin` directory (e.g., `C:\src\flutter\bin`).

4. **Run Flutter Doctor**:

- o Open Command Prompt and run the command `flutter doctor`. This command checks your environment for any dependencies you need to install, such as Android Studio and Xcode (for macOS users).

- o Follow the prompts to install any missing dependencies.

---

2. Installing Flutter on macOS

1. **Download Flutter SDK**:

28

o Visit flutter.dev and download the stable Flutter SDK for macOS.

2. **Extract the Flutter SDK**:

o Extract the contents of the downloaded zip file to a directory on your macOS, such as /flutter.

3. **Update Your Path**:

o Open a terminal and add the Flutter tool to your path by running:

```
bash
```

```
export
PATH="$PATH:`pwd`/flutter/bin"
```

o To make this change permanent, add the command to your shell's configuration file (.bash_profile or .zshrc).

4. **Run Flutter Doctor**:

o In the terminal, run flutter doctor to check the installation. If there are any missing dependencies, Flutter Doctor will guide you on how to install them.

---

3. Installing Flutter on Linux

1. **Download Flutter SDK**:

o   Go to <u>flutter.dev</u> and download the stable Flutter SDK for Linux.

2. **Extract the Flutter SDK**:

o   Extract the zip file into an appropriate directory, such as `/home/your-username/flutter`.

3. **Update Your Path**:

o   Add the `flutter/bin` directory to your PATH by running the following command in the terminal:

```bash

export
PATH="$PATH:`pwd`/flutter/bin"
```

o   To make this change permanent, you can add it to your `.bashrc` or `.zshrc` file.

4. **Run Flutter Doctor**:

o   In the terminal, run `flutter doctor` to check for any missing dependencies.

Setting Up Android Studio, Visual Studio Code, and Other Tools

After installing the Flutter SDK, you need to set up your Integrated Development Environment (IDE). Flutter supports both **Android Studio** and **Visual Studio Code (VS Code)**. Below are the steps to set up these tools:

1. Setting Up Android Studio

1. **Install Android Studio**:
   - o Download and install Android Studio from the official Android developer site.
   - o Android Studio is a full-featured IDE for Android development, and it includes everything you need to develop Flutter apps, including Android SDK, virtual devices (emulators), and other essential tools.

2. **Install Flutter and Dart Plugins**:
   - o Open Android Studio and go to the **Plugins** section in the **Preferences** menu.
   - o Search for **Flutter** and click **Install**. This will also install the **Dart** plugin, which is essential for Flutter development.

3. **Set Up an Emulator**:
   - o In Android Studio, navigate to the **AVD Manager** and create a new **Android Virtual Device (AVD)**. Select your desired device configuration and download the necessary system images.
   - o Once the emulator is set up, you can use it to run your Flutter apps.

4. **Run Flutter Doctor**:

o After installing Android Studio and the necessary plugins, run `flutter doctor` to ensure everything is set up correctly. This command checks if all required dependencies, like Android SDK, are installed.

2. Setting Up Visual Studio Code

1. **Install Visual Studio Code**:
   o Download and install Visual Studio Code from the official website.
   o Visual Studio Code is a lightweight and fast code editor that is well-suited for Flutter development.

2. **Install Flutter and Dart Extensions**:
   o Open Visual Studio Code and go to the **Extensions** view.
   o Search for **Flutter** and **Dart**, then click **Install** to add both extensions. These extensions provide syntax highlighting, debugging support, and other useful features for Flutter development.

3. **Run Flutter Doctor**:
   o As with Android Studio, run `flutter doctor` to check that Visual Studio Code is correctly configured and that the necessary tools are installed.

3. Setting Up Other Tools

- **Xcode (for iOS development)**: If you are developing for iOS, you need to install Xcode on macOS. You can download it from the **Mac App Store**. Xcode provides the tools necessary to run your app on an iOS simulator or a real device.

- **CocoaPods (for iOS dependencies)**: After installing Xcode, you may need to install CocoaPods for managing iOS dependencies. Run the following command:

```nginx
sudo gem install cocoapods
```

First App Setup: "Hello World" in Flutter

Now that your development environment is set up, it's time to create your first Flutter app. Follow these steps to create a simple "Hello World" app:

1. Create a New Flutter Project

1. **Using Android Studio**:

- o Open Android Studio and select **Start a new Flutter project**.
- o Choose **Flutter Application** and click **Next**.
- o Enter your project name, location, and description, then click **Finish**.

2. **Using Visual Studio Code**:

- o Open Visual Studio Code and use the **Flutter: New Project** command from the Command Palette (Ctrl + Shift + P).
- o Choose **Flutter Application**, name your project, and select the location.

---

2. Modify the Main Dart File

Open the lib/main.dart file and modify it to display a simple "Hello World" message. Replace the default code with the following:

dart

```
import 'package:flutter/material.dart';

void main() {
  runApp(MyApp());
}
```

```
class MyApp extends StatelessWidget {
  @override
  Widget build(BuildContext context) {
    return MaterialApp(
      home: Scaffold(
        appBar: AppBar(
          title: Text('Hello World App'),
        ),
        body: Center(
          child:  Text('Hello,  World!',  style:
TextStyle(fontSize: 24)),
        ),
      ),
    );
  }
}
```

3. Run Your App

1. **Using Android Studio**:
   - Select an Android emulator or connected device from the toolbar.
   - Click the **Run** button (green play icon) to start the app.
2. **Using Visual Studio Code**:
   - Open the terminal in VS Code and run the following command:

```arduino
flutter run
```

- o Select the device you want to run the app on (emulator or connected device).

---

4. See the Output

Once the app is running, you should see a simple screen with the text "Hello, World!" displayed in the center. Congratulations, you've successfully set up Flutter and created your first app!

Conclusion

With your development environment set up and your first Flutter app running, you're ready to begin building more complex applications. In the next chapters, you'll learn how to build layouts, manage state, and interact with APIs using Flutter. By following these steps, you've laid the groundwork for a successful Flutter development journey.

CHAPTER 4

FLUTTER ARCHITECTURE

Understanding Flutter's Architecture (Dart, Widgets, Flutter Engine)

Flutter is built on a layered architecture designed to provide both high performance and flexibility. It consists of three primary components that work together to deliver smooth, responsive apps: **Dart**, **Widgets**, and the **Flutter Engine**. Understanding each of these components is essential to fully grasp how Flutter works.

1. Dart: The Programming Language

Dart is the programming language used to build Flutter apps. It was developed by Google and is designed to be fast, modern, and easy to learn, making it an ideal choice for Flutter. Dart compiles into native code, which allows Flutter apps to achieve high performance on both Android and iOS. Here are the key points about Dart in Flutter:

- **Ahead-of-Time (AOT) Compilation**: Dart's AOT compilation allows Flutter apps to be compiled into native machine code before they are deployed, which significantly improves app startup time and overall performance.
- **Just-in-Time (JIT) Compilation**: During development, Dart uses JIT compilation, which enables **hot reload**. This allows developers to see changes in real-time without restarting the app.
- **Object-Oriented**: Dart is an object-oriented language, which makes it easy to work with classes, objects, and other familiar programming constructs.

---

2. Widgets: The Building Blocks of Flutter

At the heart of Flutter's architecture are **Widgets**. Everything in a Flutter app is a widget, from simple UI elements like buttons and text fields to complex structures like layouts and animations. In Flutter, **widgets** describe the configuration of the UI and how it should look and behave.

- **Stateless Widgets**: These are widgets that don't change over time. They don't maintain any mutable state and are purely dependent on the configuration passed to them. Examples include `Text`, `Icon`, and `Container` widgets.

Example of a Stateless Widget:

```dart
class MyApp extends StatelessWidget {
  @override
  Widget build(BuildContext context) {
    return MaterialApp(
      home: Scaffold(
        appBar:                AppBar(title:
Text("Stateless Widget")),
        body:  Center(child:  Text("Hello,
Flutter!")),
      ),
    );
  }
}
```

- **Stateful Widgets**: These are widgets that can change during the lifetime of the app. They can maintain state, allowing them to update and re-render based on user interactions or other triggers. Examples include `TextField`, `Checkbox`, and custom interactive widgets.

Example of a Stateful Widget:

```dart
class CounterApp extends StatefulWidget {
```

```
  @override
  _CounterAppState        createState()        =>
_CounterAppState();
}


class          _CounterAppState          extends
State<CounterApp> {
  int _counter = 0;

  void _incrementCounter() {
    setState(() {
      _counter++;
    });
  }

  @override
  Widget build(BuildContext context) {
    return MaterialApp(
      home: Scaffold(
        appBar:                AppBar(title:
Text("Stateful Widget")),
        body: Center(
          child: Column(
            mainAxisAlignment:
MainAxisAlignment.center,
              children: <Widget>[
                Text("Counter: $_counter"),
                ElevatedButton(
```

```
                onPressed:
_incrementCounter,
                child: Text("Increment"),
            ),
        ],
      ),
    ),
  ),
);
  }
}
```

In addition to **Stateless** and **Stateful** widgets, Flutter has other types of widgets such as **InheritedWidget**, **Provider**, and **StreamBuilder** for managing data flow and state within your app.

---

3. Flutter Engine: The Core of Flutter's Performance

The **Flutter Engine** is the low-level core that powers Flutter apps. It is written in **C++** and provides the necessary infrastructure for Flutter to interact with the device's underlying platform. The engine is responsible for rendering the UI, managing the app's lifecycle, and handling many platform-specific tasks. Here's a breakdown of its components:

- **Skia Graphics Engine**: The Flutter Engine uses Skia, a 2D graphics library, to render all graphical elements on the screen. This allows Flutter to achieve high-quality rendering and smooth animations across platforms.

- **Dart Runtime**: The engine includes a runtime for executing Dart code. The Dart runtime provides the necessary environment to run your Flutter apps.

- **Platform Channels**: The engine facilitates communication between Flutter's Dart code and native platform code (e.g., Android or iOS) through **platform channels**. This allows Flutter to access device-specific features like the camera, GPS, or sensors.

In short, the Flutter Engine ensures that the UI you design in Flutter is rendered efficiently and consistently on both Android and iOS devices.

The Role of Widgets in Flutter

Widgets are the fundamental building blocks of Flutter apps. They define everything in the app's UI, including the layout, appearance, and behavior. Flutter follows a declarative programming model, where the UI is built by combining widgets in a tree-like structure.

- **Widget Tree**: In Flutter, UI elements are arranged in a tree structure. Each widget represents a part of the user interface, and each widget can have child widgets. This widget tree is built recursively, with the root widget containing sub-widgets, and so on.

- **Declarative UI**: Flutter's approach to UI development is declarative, meaning you describe the UI and its state, and Flutter handles the rendering. For example, instead of manually updating the UI elements, you simply change the state, and Flutter takes care of updating the UI accordingly.

- **Reactivity**: Flutter's **reactive framework** means that when an app's state changes, only the parts of the UI that need to be updated are rebuilt. This makes Flutter efficient in terms of performance, as it avoids unnecessary rendering of the entire widget tree.

- **Composition**: Widgets in Flutter are composed to form more complex UIs. For instance, you can combine a `Column`, `Row`, and `Container` to create a sophisticated layout. By combining simple widgets, you can create powerful and flexible UIs without the need for complex configurations.

Hot Reload and Its Importance in Development

One of the standout features of Flutter is **hot reload**. Hot reload allows you to instantly see changes in your app's code without restarting the entire app or losing its current state. This feature significantly improves developer productivity, especially when making UI changes, debugging, or experimenting with new features.

Here's how hot reload benefits Flutter development:

- **Instant Feedback**: With hot reload, you can make changes to the app's code, such as modifying the layout or logic, and immediately see the result without restarting the app. This is particularly useful for UI development, as it allows for rapid iteration.
- **Preserving State**: Unlike traditional app development, where a full restart often resets the app state, hot reload preserves the current state of the app. This means you don't lose data or progress while testing changes.
- **Faster Debugging**: Hot reload allows you to quickly identify and fix issues by seeing the effect of your changes in real-time. It also speeds up the debugging process, as you don't have to go through the slow process of rebuilding the entire app.
- **Better Experimentation**: With hot reload, you can experiment with different UI layouts or features without worrying about the time it takes to restart the app. This encourages a more creative and exploratory approach to development.

Conclusion

Understanding Flutter's architecture is essential for building high-quality, performant apps. At its core, Flutter is powered by Dart, its flexible widget system, and the highly efficient Flutter engine. Widgets play a central role in defining the UI, and Flutter's declarative programming model allows for efficient and dynamic user interfaces. Hot reload further enhances the development process by allowing for rapid iteration and testing of changes.

By mastering Flutter's architecture and leveraging these powerful tools, you can develop cross-platform apps that perform seamlessly on both Android and iOS devices.

CHAPTER 5

UNDERSTANDING DART PROGRAMMING LANGUAGE

Basics of Dart (Variables, Functions, Data Types)

Dart is the programming language used to build Flutter applications. It is an object-oriented, class-based language with C-style syntax, making it relatively easy to learn for developers familiar with languages like Java, C#, or JavaScript. Let's explore the basics of Dart, starting with variables, functions, and data types.

1. Variables

Variables in Dart are used to store data values. Dart uses type inference, meaning it can automatically determine the type of a variable based on its value. You can also explicitly declare a variable's type.

- **Declaring Variables**:
    - o **Type Inference**: Dart automatically infers the type based on the assigned value.

46

```dart
var name = "John";    // Dart infers
that 'name' is a String
var age = 30;         // Dart infers
that 'age' is an int
```

- **Explicit Type Declaration**: You can explicitly specify the type of the variable.

```dart
String name = "John";
int age = 30;
```

- **Constants**: Use `const` or `final` for values that should not change.
  - **final**: The value can only be set once but is determined at runtime.

```dart
final double pi = 3.14;
```

  - **const**: The value is a compile-time constant.

```dart
const double gravity = 9.8;
```

2. Functions

Functions in Dart are blocks of reusable code that perform a specific task. Functions can accept parameters and return values. Dart allows you to define functions in a very flexible way.

- **Basic Function**:

dart

```
int add(int a, int b) {
  return a + b;
}
```

- **Arrow Syntax (for single-line functions)**:

dart

```
int add(int a, int b) => a + b;
```

- **Optional Parameters**: Dart supports both **named** and **positional** optional parameters.
  - **Positional Optional Parameters**:

    dart

    ```
    String greet(String name, [String greeting = "Hello"]) {
      return "$greeting, $name!";
    }
    ```

o **Named Optional Parameters**:

```dart
String greet({String name = "Guest",
String greeting = "Hello"}) {
  return "$greeting, $name!";
}
```

- **Returning Functions**: Dart supports higher-order functions, meaning you can return a function from another function.

```dart
Function multiply(int a) {
  return (int b) => a * b;
}
var multiplyByTwo = multiply(2);
print(multiplyByTwo(3));  // Outputs: 6
```

3. Data Types

Dart has several built-in data types, including numbers, strings, booleans, lists, sets, and maps.

- **Numbers**: Dart supports both integer (int) and floating-point (double) numbers.

49

```dart
int x = 10;
double y = 3.14;
```

- **Strings**: Strings are enclosed in either single or double quotes.

```dart
String message = "Hello, Dart!";
String multiline = '''
This is
a multiline
string.
''';
```

- **Booleans**: The `bool` type holds the values `true` or `false`.

```dart
bool isActive = true;
```

- **Lists**: Dart has both fixed-size and growable lists.

```dart
List<int> numbers = [1, 2, 3];
```

```
numbers.add(4);  // Adds an element to the
list
```

- **Sets**: A collection of unique elements.

```dart
```

```dart
Set<String> fruits = {"apple", "banana",
"orange"};
```

- **Maps**: A collection of key-value pairs.

```dart
```

```dart
Map<String, int> ageMap = {"Alice": 25,
"Bob": 30};
```

Object-Oriented Programming in Dart

Dart is an object-oriented language, which means it revolves around the concepts of classes and objects. In Dart, everything is an object, and you can use classes to create your own data types.

---

1. Classes and Objects

A **class** is a blueprint for creating objects, and an **object** is an instance of a class.

- **Defining a Class**:

```dart
class Person {
  String name;
  int age;

  // Constructor
  Person(this.name, this.age);

  // Method
  void introduce() {
    print("Hi, I'm $name and I'm $age years
old.");
  }
}

// Creating an object of the Person class
var person = Person("Alice", 25);
person.introduce();   // Outputs: Hi, I'm
Alice and I'm 25 years old.
```

- **Constructor**: Constructors are special methods used to initialize objects. Dart provides a shorthand constructor syntax that initializes variables directly.

```dart
class Car {
```

```
String model;
int year;

Car(this.model,    this.year);         //
Constructor shorthand
}
```

- **Getters and Setters**: Dart allows you to define custom getters and setters to control access to an object's properties.

```
dart

class Circle {
  double radius;

  Circle(this.radius);

  // Getter for area
  double get area => 3.14 * radius *
radius;

  // Setter for radius
  set setRadius(double r) => radius = r;
}
```

2. Inheritance and Polymorphism

- **Inheritance**: Dart allows one class to inherit from another. The child class inherits the properties and methods of the parent class, which promotes code reuse.

```dart
class Animal {
  void speak() {
    print("Animal makes a sound");
  }
}

class Dog extends Animal {
  @override
  void speak() {
    print("Dog barks");
  }
}

var dog = Dog();
dog.speak();  // Outputs: Dog barks
```

- **Polymorphism**: Dart supports polymorphism, which allows you to use the same method name to perform different tasks depending on the object type.

```dart
void makeSound(Animal animal) {
```

```
    animal.speak();
}

var dog = Dog();
makeSound(dog);   // Outputs: Dog barks
```

3. Interfaces and Abstract Classes

- **Interfaces**: Dart does not have a specific keyword for interfaces. Instead, any class can serve as an interface.

```dart
class Animal {
  void speak();
}

class Dog implements Animal {
  @override
  void speak() {
    print("Dog barks");
  }
}
```

- **Abstract Classes**: Abstract classes cannot be instantiated directly. They are meant to be extended by other classes.

```dart
```

```
abstract class Shape {
  double area();
}

class Circle extends Shape {
  double radius;

  Circle(this.radius);

  @override
  double area() => 3.14 * radius * radius;
}
```

Asynchronous Programming in Dart

Asynchronous programming is a fundamental concept in Dart that allows you to perform non-blocking operations, such as network requests or file I/O, without freezing the app's UI. Dart provides several tools for asynchronous programming, including `Future`, `async`, and `await`.

1. Futures

A **Future** represents a value that might not be available yet but will be available at some point in the future. You can think of it as a placeholder for a result that will be computed asynchronously.

- **Using Future**:

dart

```
Future<String> fetchData() async {
  return  Future.delayed(Duration(seconds:
2), () => "Data loaded");
}

void main() async {
  var data = await fetchData();
  print(data);  // Outputs: Data loaded
}
```

- **Future Chaining**: You can chain multiple `Future` calls using `.then()` or `await`.

dart

```
Future<String> fetchData() async {
  return  Future.delayed(Duration(seconds:
1), () => "Data");
}

Future<void> processData() async {
  var data = await fetchData();
  print("Processed $data");
}
```

2. Async and Await

The `async` keyword is used to mark a function as asynchronous, and the `await` keyword is used to pause execution until a `Future` is complete.

- **Using async and await**:

```dart
Future<String> fetchData() async {
  await   Future.delayed(Duration(seconds:
2));
  return "Data fetched";
}

void main() async {
  var data = await fetchData();
  print(data);   // Outputs: Data fetched
}
```

---

3. Streams

A **Stream** is a sequence of asynchronous events. Unlike a `Future`, which returns a single result, a `Stream` provides multiple results over time (e.g., incoming data from a network).

- **Listening to Streams**:

```dart
dart

Stream<int> countToFive() async* {
  for (var i = 1; i <= 5; i++) {
    await Future.delayed(Duration(seconds:
1));
    yield i;
  }
}

void main() {
  countToFive().listen((data) {
    print(data);   // Outputs: 1, 2, 3, 4,
5 (each on a new line)
  });
}
```

Conclusion

Dart is a powerful, easy-to-learn programming language that provides the core foundation for Flutter app development. Its support for object-oriented programming, asynchronous programming with `Future`, `async/await`, and streams, combined with its modern syntax, makes Dart an ideal choice for building responsive and high-performance mobile apps. By understanding Dart's basics, object-oriented principles, and asynchronous capabilities, you'll be well-equipped to write efficient and effective Flutter applications.

CHAPTER 6

THE FLUTTER WIDGET TREE

Understanding the Widget Tree Structure

In Flutter, **everything is a widget.** A widget in Flutter is a description of the part of the user interface (UI) that should be rendered. These widgets are organized in a hierarchical tree structure, known as the **widget tree**, which defines the layout and visual structure of the app.

The widget tree is built using **parent-child relationships**. A widget can have one or more child widgets, and those child widgets can have their own children, creating a tree-like structure. The root of the widget tree is typically the main widget of the app, and all other widgets are nested underneath it.

Key Concepts of the Widget Tree:

1. **Root Widget**: The top-level widget that contains the entire app. Typically, this is the `MaterialApp` widget (for Material Design apps) or `CupertinoApp` (for iOS-styled apps).

```dart
void main() {
  runApp(MyApp());
}

class MyApp extends StatelessWidget {
  @override
  Widget build(BuildContext context) {
    return MaterialApp(
      title: 'Flutter Demo',
      home: MyHomePage(),
    );
  }
}
```

2. **Parent-Child Relationship**: Widgets can contain other widgets as their children. For example, a Column widget can contain multiple Text widgets as its children.

```dart
Column(
  children: <Widget>[
    Text('First Item'),
    Text('Second Item'),
  ],
);
```

61

3. **Composition**: Flutter's UI is built by composing widgets together. Instead of subclassing widgets for specific use cases, you compose a variety of widgets to create custom interfaces.

```dart
Container(
  padding: EdgeInsets.all(16),
  child: Column(
    children: <Widget>[
      Text('Hello, Flutter!'),
      RaisedButton(onPressed:      ()      {},
child: Text('Press Me')),
    ],
  ),
);
```

Widget Tree Example: A simple widget tree might look like this:

```scss
MyApp (StatelessWidget)
  └─ MaterialApp (Widget)
      └─ Scaffold (Widget)
          ├─ AppBar (Widget)
          └─ Column (Widget)
              ├─ Text (Widget)
```

62

```
├── RaisedButton (Widget)
```

Each widget in the tree has its own properties and configuration, and Flutter uses this tree to efficiently render the UI.

Stateless vs. Stateful Widgets

In Flutter, widgets are categorized into **Stateless Widgets** and **Stateful Widgets**, depending on whether or not they need to manage mutable state. Understanding the difference between the two is crucial for building dynamic and responsive apps.

1. Stateless Widgets

A **StatelessWidget** is a widget that doesn't change over time. Its state is fixed once it is built, and it doesn't hold any mutable data that can trigger a rebuild. Stateless widgets are ideal for displaying static content or information that doesn't require interaction or updates.

- **Example of StatelessWidget**:

```dart
class MyHomePage extends StatelessWidget {
  @override
```

```
Widget build(BuildContext context) {
  return Scaffold(
    appBar:                    AppBar(title:
Text('Stateless Widget')),
      body: Center(child: Text('This is a
stateless widget!')),
    );
  }
}
```

Since Stateless widgets are static, they do not require a **state object**. The UI is constructed once and remains unchanged throughout the widget's lifecycle.

---

2. Stateful Widgets

A **StatefulWidget** is a widget that can change its appearance based on changes in its state. Unlike Stateless widgets, Stateful widgets can hold mutable state, which means they can rebuild when the state changes. This makes Stateful widgets suitable for user interactions or dynamic data updates.

Stateful widgets are composed of two classes:

- **StatefulWidget**: The widget class itself. It only defines the **configuration** and **structure** of the widget.

- **State**: A separate class that holds the **mutable state** and defines the logic for how the widget should be updated when the state changes.
- **Example of StatefulWidget**:

```dart
class CounterApp extends StatefulWidget {
  @override
  _CounterAppState    createState()      =>
_CounterAppState();
}

class       _CounterAppState       extends
State<CounterApp> {
  int _counter = 0;

  void _incrementCounter() {
    setState(() {
      _counter++;
    });
  }

  @override
  Widget build(BuildContext context) {
    return Scaffold(
      appBar: AppBar(title: Text('Stateful
Widget')),
      body: Center(
```

```
      child: Column(
        mainAxisAlignment:
MainAxisAlignment.center,
          children: <Widget>[
            Text('Counter: $_counter'),
            RaisedButton(
              onPressed:
_incrementCounter,
              child: Text('Increment'),
            ),
          ],
        ),
      ),
    );
  }
}
```

In this example, the _counter is a mutable piece of state, and the setState method triggers a rebuild whenever the state changes (in this case, when the button is pressed).

Differences Between Stateless and Stateful Widgets:

Feature	Stateless Widget	Stateful Widget
State	Cannot change once built.	Can change during the app's lifetime.
Rebuild	Rebuilt only when parent widget rebuilds.	Can rebuild independently when state changes.
Use Case	Used for static content, e.g., labels or static UI.	Used for dynamic content, e.g., interactive buttons, forms.
Performance	Generally faster as they don't require frequent rebuilding.	Slightly slower as they may require more frequent rebuilds.

How the Widget Tree Impacts Performance and Rendering

The widget tree is crucial for Flutter's performance and rendering, and understanding how it works can help you build more efficient apps.

1. Efficient Rendering with the Widget Tree

Flutter uses a highly optimized rendering pipeline. The widget tree is the starting point for the rendering process. When a widget is rebuilt (for example, when the state of a StatefulWidget changes), Flutter rebuilds only the affected portion of the tree, rather than the entire UI. This makes Flutter highly efficient compared to other frameworks that might redraw the entire screen.

- **Widget vs. Element**: In Flutter, widgets are immutable, meaning once created, they don't change. However, Flutter uses a corresponding **Element** for each widget, which is mutable and manages the widget's lifecycle. When the state changes, only the affected elements are updated, minimizing unnecessary work.
- **The Rendering Process**: Flutter's rendering process involves the following steps:
    1. **Build Phase**: The widget tree is built using `build()` methods.
    2. **Element Tree**: Each widget is associated with an **Element** that manages its lifecycle and updates.
    3. **Render Tree**: This tree contains **RenderObjects**, which are responsible for painting and layout. Flutter uses this tree to render the UI on the screen.

---

2. Impact of Frequent Rebuilds on Performance

68

Frequent rebuilds can affect performance, especially if the widget tree is deep or if complex widgets are being constantly updated. When a widget rebuilds, it re-renders its entire subtree, which can be costly if not managed correctly. Flutter's **widget tree** is optimized to minimize this by only rebuilding widgets that have actually changed, but **overusing stateful widgets** or **inefficiently managing state** can lead to performance issues.

3. Best Practices for Optimizing Performance

- **Use Stateless Widgets When Possible**: Since StatelessWidgets don't rebuild unless their parent rebuilds, they are more efficient for static parts of the UI. Try to use them wherever you don't need to manage mutable state.

- **Use `const` Constructors**: If a widget doesn't depend on any dynamic data, marking it as `const` tells Flutter that the widget never changes. Flutter can then optimize the widget and reuse it instead of rebuilding it from scratch.

  dart

  ```dart
  const Text('This is a constant text');
  ```

- **Limit the Scope of Rebuilds**: Use `setState` efficiently by only changing the state that needs to be updated. Avoid calling `setState` for things that don't affect the UI, as it triggers a rebuild of the widget tree.

- **Leverage `ListView.builder` for Large Lists**: When dealing with large or dynamic lists, use `ListView.builder` instead of `ListView` to lazily load items. This ensures only the visible items are rendered, which saves memory and improves performance.

Conclusion

The widget tree is a fundamental concept in Flutter's architecture, and understanding how it works is crucial for creating efficient, high-performance apps. By distinguishing between Stateless and Stateful widgets and learning how Flutter renders the widget tree, you can optimize your app's performance and ensure smooth user experiences. Keep the widget tree shallow when possible, use StatelessWidgets for static content, and be mindful of unnecessary rebuilds to keep your app running smoothly.

CHAPTER 7

LAYOUTS IN FLUTTER

Introduction to Flutter's Layout System

Flutter provides a flexible and powerful layout system that enables developers to build highly responsive UIs. The layout system is based on the concept of **widgets** that describe the visual structure of the UI. Each widget can either be a container for other widgets (such as a `Column` or `Row`) or a visual element that displays content (like `Text` or `Image`).

At its core, Flutter's layout system works through the concept of **parent-child relationships** between widgets. A parent widget arranges its children according to its layout constraints, which results in a visually structured UI.

Flutter follows a **flexible, box-based layout model**, where each widget defines how much space it wants to occupy and how it should be aligned. The basic principle is that every widget has constraints that determine its size, and it must fit within those constraints.

Key Concepts in Flutter's Layout System:

- **Constraints**: Widgets are given constraints from their parent widgets. These constraints dictate how much space the widget can take up in the layout. A widget may request a certain size (e.g., a button that needs 100x50 pixels), but the parent widget will decide whether that request fits within its own size.

- **Sizing**: Widgets define their size based on their constraints. If the widget has a fixed size, like a Container with a width and height, it will occupy that exact amount of space. However, some widgets (like Text) are flexible and take up only as much space as required to display their content.

- **Alignment**: Widgets can also define how their children should be aligned within the available space. Flutter provides multiple alignment options like top-left, center, or bottom-right.

- **Flex and Expanded**: Flutter allows for flexible layouts using Row, Column, and Flex widgets. These widgets enable you to define how children should share available space within their parent widget.

Common Layout Widgets (Column, Row, Stack, GridView)

Flutter provides several layout widgets that help organize and arrange child widgets in different ways. Let's look at the most commonly used layout widgets.

---

1. Column (Vertical Layout)

The `Column` widget arranges its children vertically. Each child widget is laid out one below the other. It is commonly used for stacking widgets in a vertical direction, like text fields, buttons, or images.

- **Basic Example**:

```dart
Column(
  children: <Widget>[
    Text('Hello'),
    Text('Flutter'),
    ElevatedButton(onPressed:    ()    {},
child: Text('Press Me')),
  ],
);
```

- **Key Properties**:

○ `mainAxisAlignment`: Controls how children are aligned along the main axis (vertical in the case of a `Column`).

○ `crossAxisAlignment`: Controls the alignment along the cross axis (horizontal in the case of a `Column`).

○ `children`: A list of widgets arranged vertically.

- **Example with Alignment**:

```dart
dart

Column(
  mainAxisAlignment:
MainAxisAlignment.center,    // Vertically
centered
  crossAxisAlignment:
CrossAxisAlignment.start, // Horizontally
aligned to the start
  children: <Widget>[
    Text('First Text'),
    Text('Second Text'),
  ],
);
```

2. Row (Horizontal Layout)

The `Row` widget arranges its children horizontally. Each child widget is placed side by side. It's commonly used for horizontal layouts like icons, buttons, and text elements aligned in a row.

- **Basic Example**:

```dart
Row(
  children: <Widget>[
    Icon(Icons.home),
    Text('Home'),
    ElevatedButton(onPressed:    ()    {},
child: Text('Go')),
  ],
);
```

- **Key Properties**:
  - `mainAxisAlignment`: Aligns children along the main axis (horizontal in the case of a `Row`).
  - `crossAxisAlignment`: Aligns children along the cross axis (vertical in the case of a `Row`).
  - `children`: A list of widgets arranged horizontally.
- **Example with Spacing**:

```dart
Row(
```

```
      mainAxisAlignment:
MainAxisAlignment.spaceEvenly,    //    Even
space between elements
    children: <Widget>[
      Icon(Icons.home),
      Icon(Icons.search),
      Icon(Icons.notifications),
    ],
  );
```

3. Stack (Overlapping Layout)

The Stack widget allows you to place widgets on top of each other. It's useful when you want to create overlapping UI elements, like placing a text label over an image.

- **Basic Example**:

dart

```
Stack(
  children: <Widget>[
    Image.asset('assets/background.jpg'),
    Positioned(
      top: 20,
      left: 20,
      child: Text('Hello, Stack!'),
    ),
```

```
  ],
);
```

- **Key Properties**:
  - children: A list of widgets that are stacked on top of each other.
  - Positioned: A widget that allows you to position children within a Stack using top, left, right, and bottom properties.
- **Example with Positioned**:

dart

```
Stack(
  children: <Widget>[
    Container(color: Colors.blue, height:
200, width: 200),
    Positioned(
      top: 50,
      left: 50,
      child:              Container(color:
Colors.white, height: 100, width: 100),
    ),
  ],
);
```

4. GridView (Grid Layout)

The GridView widget creates a grid layout where items are arranged in rows and columns. It is commonly used to display items such as images, cards, or product listings in a grid format.

- **Basic Example**:

dart

```
GridView.count(
  crossAxisCount: 2, // Two columns
  children: <Widget>[
    Container(color: Colors.blue, height:
100, width: 100),
    Container(color: Colors.red, height:
100, width: 100),
    Container(color: Colors.green, height:
100, width: 100),
  ],
);
```

- **Key Properties**:
  - crossAxisCount: Defines how many columns you want in the grid.
  - children: A list of widgets arranged in the grid.
- **Example with GridView.builder** (for large or dynamic data):

dart

```
GridView.builder(
  gridDelegate:
SliverGridDelegateWithFixedCrossAxisCount
(
    crossAxisCount: 3,
  ),
  itemCount: 20,
  itemBuilder: (context, index) {
    return Card(
      child:    Center(child:    Text('Item
$index')),
    );
  },
);
```

Building Responsive UIs with Flutter

Building responsive UIs is critical to ensure that your app looks great on devices with different screen sizes and orientations. Flutter offers several tools and techniques to make your UI responsive.

1. Using MediaQuery

MediaQuery allows you to retrieve information about the current device's screen size, orientation, and other properties. You can use this information to adjust your layout based on the screen dimensions.

- **Example**:

```dart
var              width              =
MediaQuery.of(context).size.width;
var              height             =
MediaQuery.of(context).size.height;

return Scaffold(
  body: Center(
    child: Container(
      width: width * 0.8, // 80% of the
screen width
      height: height * 0.5, // 50% of the
screen height
      color: Colors.blue,
    ),
  ),
);
```

- **Example for Landscape and Portrait**:

```dart
var              orientation        =
MediaQuery.of(context).orientation;
```

```
if (orientation == Orientation.portrait) {
  // Build portrait layout
} else {
  // Build landscape layout
}
```

2. LayoutBuilder

`LayoutBuilder` is another powerful widget that provides the parent widget's constraints, allowing you to build layouts that adapt based on the available space. It is particularly useful when you need to build layouts that change dynamically depending on the available space.

- **Example**:

dart

```
LayoutBuilder(
  builder: (context, constraints) {
    if (constraints.maxWidth > 600) {
      return Row(
        children: <Widget>[
          Expanded(child: Container(color:
Colors.blue)),
          Expanded(child: Container(color:
Colors.red)),
        ],
```

```
    );
  } else {
    return Column(
      children: <Widget>[
        Container(color:     Colors.blue,
height: 100),
        Container(color:       Colors.red,
height: 100),
      ],
    );
  }
},
);
```

3. Flex and Expanded Widgets

The `Flex` and `Expanded` widgets allow you to create flexible layouts that adjust based on the screen size. You can use these widgets in `Column` or `Row` to distribute space evenly or proportionally.

- **Example**:

```dart

Row(
  children: <Widget>[
```

```
        Expanded(child:        Container(color:
Colors.green, height: 100)),
        Expanded(child:        Container(color:
Colors.orange, height: 100)),
    ],
);
```

- **Proportional Layout**:

```dart
dart

Row(
  children: <Widget>[
    Expanded(flex:           2,           child:
Container(color: Colors.green)),
    Expanded(flex:           1,           child:
Container(color: Colors.orange)),
    ],
);
```

Conclusion

Flutter provides a robust layout system that allows developers to create flexible and adaptive user interfaces. By understanding the common layout widgets like Column, Row, Stack, and GridView, as well as how to build responsive UIs using tools like MediaQuery, LayoutBuilder, and Flex, you can create dynamic apps that work seamlessly on a variety of screen sizes and orientations.

Responsive design is crucial for ensuring that your app looks good and functions well on both small and large devices. Using Flutter's powerful layout system, you can easily build beautiful, scalable, and responsive mobile apps.

CHAPTER 8

NAVIGATING BETWEEN SCREENS

How to Implement Navigation in Flutter

Navigation is a key aspect of app development, as it allows users to move between different screens or views. Flutter provides a simple and flexible navigation system to handle routing and managing screen transitions. The primary navigation mechanism in Flutter involves using the **Navigator** widget, which manages a stack of screens (or **routes**) and allows you to push or pop them onto/from the stack.

The core navigation methods in Flutter are:

- **push**: Adds a new route to the navigation stack (a new screen).
- **pop**: Removes the current route from the stack (goes back to the previous screen).
- **pushReplacement**: Replaces the current route with a new one.

1. Basic Navigation with `Navigator`

The most basic form of navigation in Flutter involves using the `Navigator` widget to push a new screen and pop the current one.

- **Navigating to a new screen**:

dart

```
Navigator.push(
   context,
   MaterialPageRoute(builder:  (context)  =>
SecondScreen()),
   );
```

- **Returning to the previous screen**:

dart

```
Navigator.pop(context);
```

In the above example, `MaterialPageRoute` is used to define the new screen, and the `push` method adds this screen to the navigation stack. `pop` is used to return to the previous screen.

---

2. Using `MaterialPageRoute` for Basic Transitions

`MaterialPageRoute` is one of the default route types used in Flutter to create transitions between screens. It provides a simple transition animation, but you can also define custom transitions if needed.

- **Basic example of navigating to a new screen**:

```dart
Navigator.push(
  context,
  MaterialPageRoute(builder: (context) =>
SecondScreen()),
);
```

In this case, `MaterialPageRoute` creates a default sliding transition to the new screen.

Using Routes and Named Routes

Named routes are a way of defining routes with a string identifier. This approach can simplify navigation, especially for large apps where you have many screens. With named routes, you don't need to pass the widget directly into the navigation method. Instead, you use the route's name to push or pop a screen.

---

1. Defining Routes

First, you need to define the named routes in your app's `MaterialApp` widget. You can specify a map of route names to their corresponding screen (widget) in the `routes` property.

- **Example of defining named routes**:

```dart
void main() {
  runApp(MyApp());
}

class MyApp extends StatelessWidget {
  @override
  Widget build(BuildContext context) {
    return MaterialApp(
      title: 'Flutter App',
      initialRoute: '/',
      routes: {
        '/': (context) => HomeScreen(),
        '/second':       (context)        =>
SecondScreen(),
      },
    );
  }
}
```

In the example above:

- The initial route is set to `'/'`, which means the app will start at the `HomeScreen`.
- The `SecondScreen` can be accessed using the `/second` route.

2. Navigating with Named Routes

Once you've defined your named routes, you can navigate to them using the `Navigator.pushNamed` method.

- **Navigating to a named route**:

```dart
Navigator.pushNamed(context, '/second');
```

- **Returning to the previous screen**:

```dart
Navigator.pop(context);
```

3. Passing Data with Named Routes

Named routes allow you to pass data between screens as well. This can be done by using the settings property in MaterialPageRoute or by using arguments when pushing a named route.

- **Passing data to a named route**:

dart

```
Navigator.pushNamed(
  context,
  '/second',
  arguments: 'Hello from the Home Screen!',
);
```

- **Receiving data in the destination screen**: On the receiving screen (in this case, SecondScreen), you can access the passed data using the ModalRoute.of(context)?.settings.arguments property.

dart

```
class SecondScreen extends StatelessWidget
{
  @override
  Widget build(BuildContext context) {
```

```
    final      String      message      =
ModalRoute.of(context)?.settings.argument
s as String;
    return Scaffold(
      appBar: AppBar(title:  Text('Second
Screen')),
      body: Center(child: Text(message)),
    );
  }
}
```

In the above example, we pass a `String` to the `SecondScreen` via the `arguments` property and display the received message.

Passing Data Between Screens

There are several ways to pass data between screens in Flutter. Besides using named routes and the `arguments` property, you can also pass data directly using the constructor of the destination screen, or by using **global state management solutions**.

---

1. Passing Data through Constructor

You can pass data between screens by defining a constructor in the destination screen and passing the data directly when navigating.

- **Example**:

dart

```
class SecondScreen extends StatelessWidget
{
  final String data;

  // Constructor to receive data
  SecondScreen({required this.data});

  @override
  Widget build(BuildContext context) {
    return Scaffold(
      appBar: AppBar(title: Text('Second
Screen')),
      body: Center(child: Text(data)),
    );
  }
}

// Navigating to the SecondScreen
Navigator.push(
  context,
  MaterialPageRoute(
    builder:         (context)         =>
SecondScreen(data: 'Hello from the Home
Screen!'),
  ),
);
```

In this example, the `SecondScreen` constructor takes a `String` parameter, and we pass the data directly when navigating via `MaterialPageRoute`.

2. Using `Provider` or Other State Management Solutions

For more complex applications, you may need a more robust solution for passing and managing data. This is where state management libraries like `Provider`, `Riverpod`, or `Bloc` come in. These tools allow you to manage app-wide state and pass data seamlessly between different parts of your app.

- **Using `Provider`:**

```dart
dart

class User {
  final String name;
  User(this.name);
}

// In the main app widget:
runApp(
  ChangeNotifierProvider(
    create: (context) => User('John Doe'),
    child: MyApp(),
  ),
```

```
);
```

> o You can then access and pass the data through the app using `Provider` to share and manage data across different screens.

Handling Dynamic Routes

In some cases, you may want to navigate to a screen dynamically based on the route or data. Flutter supports **dynamic routes**, where the routes are not predefined but can be handled dynamically through a `RouteFactory`.

- **Example of dynamic routes**:

dart

```dart
onGenerateRoute: (settings) {
   if (settings.name == '/user') {
     final User user = settings.arguments as
User;
     return MaterialPageRoute(
       builder:          (context)          =>
UserScreen(user: user),
     );
   }
   return null;   // Return null to use
default route handling.
```

```
},
```

This approach is useful when you want to handle specific arguments dynamically and have more control over the navigation behavior.

Conclusion

Navigation in Flutter is both simple and flexible. By using **Navigator**, **named routes**, and passing data through **constructor arguments** or **route arguments**, you can easily manage transitions between screens and pass data as needed. Flutter's routing system provides a variety of options to suit different app requirements, from basic navigation to more complex dynamic routes.

For larger applications, consider using state management solutions like **Provider** to manage and pass data seamlessly across screens. With this knowledge, you're now equipped to implement navigation in any Flutter app.

CHAPTER 9

WORKING WITH LISTS AND GRIDS

Displaying Data in a ListView and GridView

In Flutter, **ListView** and **GridView** are two of the most commonly used widgets for displaying large collections of data in a scrollable and visually organized manner. Both widgets provide flexibility in how data is displayed, allowing for single-column or multi-column layouts.

1. ListView: A Vertical List of Items

The `ListView` widget is used to display a scrolling list of widgets in a single vertical column. It's perfect for cases where you need to show a sequence of items, such as a list of text, images, or custom widgets.

- **Basic Example**:

  dart

```
ListView(
  children: <Widget>[
    ListTile(title: Text('Item 1')),
    ListTile(title: Text('Item 2')),
    ListTile(title: Text('Item 3')),
  ],
);
```

- **Key Properties**:
  - o `children`: A list of widgets to display in the list. Typically, this would be a list of `ListTile` widgets or custom widgets.
  - o **Scrolling**: If the number of children exceeds the screen size, the `ListView` automatically becomes scrollable.

---

2. GridView: A Grid of Items

The `GridView` widget is used to display a 2D array of widgets, making it ideal for situations where you want to present items in rows and columns (like a photo gallery or a collection of cards).

- **Basic Example**:

```
dart
```

```
GridView.count(
```

```
    crossAxisCount: 2, // Number of columns
in the grid
    children: <Widget>[
        Container(color: Colors.blue, height:
100, width: 100),
        Container(color: Colors.green, height:
100, width: 100),
        Container(color: Colors.red, height:
100, width: 100),
    ],
);
```

- **Key Properties**:
  - o `crossAxisCount`: The number of columns in the grid.
  - o `children`: A list of widgets to be displayed in the grid.
- **GridView.builder**: For more efficient lists, especially when the data is dynamic or large, `GridView.builder` allows you to build grid items lazily as they scroll into view, improving performance.

dart

```
GridView.builder(
  gridDelegate:
SliverGridDelegateWithFixedCrossAxisCount
(
    crossAxisCount: 3, // Number of columns
```

```
    ),
    itemCount: 20, // Total number of items
    itemBuilder: (context, index) {
      return Container(
        color: Colors.blue,
        margin: EdgeInsets.all(8),
        child:    Center(child:    Text('Item
$index')),
      );
    },
  );
```

Customizing List Items with ListTile

The `ListTile` widget is a highly customizable widget that's often used inside a `ListView` to display a single item in a list. It typically contains content such as text, images, and icons, and provides built-in support for leading, trailing, and title properties.

1. Basic ListTile Example:

dart

```
ListView(
  children: <Widget>[
    ListTile(
      leading: Icon(Icons.home),
```

```
    title: Text('Home'),
    subtitle: Text('This is the home screen'),
    trailing: Icon(Icons.arrow_forward),
    onTap: () {
      // Handle the tap event
    },
  ),
  ListTile(
    leading: Icon(Icons.settings),
    title: Text('Settings'),
    onTap: () {
      // Handle the tap event
    },
  ),
 ],
);
```

- **Key Properties of ListTile**:
  - leading: A widget that is displayed before the title, often used for icons or images.
  - title: The primary content of the list item (usually a Text widget).
  - subtitle: An optional secondary piece of information displayed below the title.
  - trailing: A widget displayed after the title, often used for icons or buttons.
  - onTap: A callback function that is called when the list item is tapped.

2. Using ListTile for Custom Items:

You can customize `ListTile` to display any kind of widget, including images, buttons, and more. For example, you can use it to create a profile card with a user's picture and name.

```dart
ListView(
  children: <Widget>[
    ListTile(
      leading: CircleAvatar(
        backgroundImage:
NetworkImage('https://example.com/profile.jpg')
,
      ),
      title: Text('John Doe'),
      subtitle: Text('Flutter Developer'),
      trailing: Icon(Icons.phone),
      onTap: () {
        // Open phone app or call
      },
    ),
  ],
);
```

Implementing Infinite Scrolling

Infinite scrolling is a technique where new data is loaded dynamically as the user scrolls to the bottom of the list. This is useful when dealing with large datasets or when data is fetched from an API. Flutter makes implementing infinite scrolling easy with `ListView.builder` and the `ScrollController`.

---

1. Basic Infinite Scrolling with ListView.builder

You can implement infinite scrolling by using `ListView.builder` and listening to the scroll position. When the user reaches the end of the list, new data is fetched and added to the list.

- **Example**:

dart

```
class InfiniteScrollList extends StatefulWidget
{
  @override
  _InfiniteScrollListState   createState()   =>
_InfiniteScrollListState();
}
```

```
class      _InfiniteScrollListState      extends
State<InfiniteScrollList> {
  List<int> _data = List.generate(30, (index) =>
index);  // Initial data
  ScrollController      _scrollController      =
ScrollController();

  @override
  void initState() {
    super.initState();

_scrollController.addListener(_scrollListener);
  }

  void _scrollListener() {
    if    (_scrollController.position.pixels    ==
_scrollController.position.maxScrollExtent) {
      _loadMoreData();
    }
  }

  void _loadMoreData() {
    // Simulate fetching more data
    Future.delayed(Duration(seconds: 2), () {
      setState(() {
        _data.addAll(List.generate(30,    (index)
=> _data.length + index));
      });
    });
```

103

```
      }

  @override
  Widget build(BuildContext context) {
    return Scaffold(
      appBar:    AppBar(title:    Text('Infinite
Scrolling')),
      body: ListView.builder(
        controller: _scrollController,
        itemCount: _data.length,
        itemBuilder: (context, index) {
          return ListTile(
            title: Text('Item ${_data[index]}'),
          );
        },
      ),
    );
  }

  @override
  void dispose() {
    _scrollController.dispose();
    super.dispose();
  }
}
```

- **Explanation**:
  - o The _scrollController listens for changes in the scroll position.

- o When the user reaches the bottom (maxScrollExtent), the _loadMoreData function is called, simulating the fetching of new data.
- o The setState function is called to update the UI with the new data.

2. Adding a Loading Indicator

When fetching new data, it's common to show a loading spinner or indicator at the bottom of the list. You can add a loading widget when new data is being fetched.

- **Example with Loading Indicator**:

```dart
class InfiniteScrollWithLoading extends
StatefulWidget {
  @override
  _InfiniteScrollWithLoadingState createState()
=> _InfiniteScrollWithLoadingState();
}

class _InfiniteScrollWithLoadingState extends
State<InfiniteScrollWithLoading> {
```

```dart
  List<int> _data = List.generate(30, (index) =>
index); // Initial data
  bool _isLoading = false;
  ScrollController      _scrollController      =
ScrollController();

  @override
  void initState() {
    super.initState();

_scrollController.addListener(_scrollListener);
  }

  void _scrollListener() {
    if   (_scrollController.position.pixels   ==
_scrollController.position.maxScrollExtent) {
      if (!_isLoading) {
        _loadMoreData();
      }
    }
  }

  void _loadMoreData() {
    setState(() {
      _isLoading = true;
    });
    // Simulate fetching more data
    Future.delayed(Duration(seconds: 2), () {
      setState(() {
```

```
        _data.addAll(List.generate(30,    (index)
=> _data.length + index));
        _isLoading = false;
      });
    });
  }


  @override
  Widget build(BuildContext context) {
    return Scaffold(
      appBar:    AppBar(title:    Text('Infinite
Scrolling with Loading')),
      body: ListView.builder(
        controller: _scrollController,
        itemCount: _data.length + 1, // +1 for
the loading indicator
        itemBuilder: (context, index) {
          if (index == _data.length) {
            return _isLoading
                ?                    Center(child:
CircularProgressIndicator())
                : SizedBox.shrink(); // Empty
space when not loading
          }
          return ListTile(
            title: Text('Item ${_data[index]}'),
          );
        },
      ),
```

```
    );
  }

@override
void dispose() {
  _scrollController.dispose();
  super.dispose();
  }
}
```

- **Explanation**:
  - When the user scrolls to the end of the list, a loading spinner is shown (`CircularProgressIndicator`).
  - `_isLoading` is used to track whether new data is being fetched to avoid triggering multiple requests.

Conclusion

Working with lists and grids is an essential part of building Flutter apps, especially when dealing with dynamic data. `ListView` and `GridView` provide efficient ways to display large amounts of data, while `ListTile` allows for customization of individual items. Implementing infinite scrolling is simple using `ListView.builder` and a `ScrollController`, making it easy to fetch new data as the user scrolls. By combining these techniques, you can create smooth, interactive, and dynamic UIs for your Flutter apps.

CHAPTER 10

MANAGING STATE IN FLUTTER

Introduction to State Management

State management is a fundamental concept in Flutter and any other framework that builds dynamic UIs. The "state" refers to any data or information that can change over time in the application, such as user input, data fetched from an API, or internal variables. In Flutter, state management involves ensuring that the UI reflects the current state of your app and responds to state changes efficiently.

Flutter offers several ways to manage state, from local state within individual widgets to more global and complex state management solutions. Understanding how to handle state effectively will help ensure your app runs smoothly, scales well, and provides a responsive user experience.

Why State Management is Important:

- **Consistency**: Keeping your app's UI consistent with its internal data.

- **Separation of Concerns**: Managing different parts of the app's logic in separate places, making it easier to maintain and scale.
- **Reactivity**: Ensuring that changes in the app's data automatically update the UI.

Different State Management Techniques

Flutter provides a wide range of state management solutions, each suited for different use cases. Below, we'll explore the most popular ones: **Provider**, **Riverpod**, **BLoC**, and **Redux**.

1. Provider

`Provider` is one of the most widely used state management solutions in Flutter. It is simple to understand and integrates well with the widget tree, making it ideal for many apps. `Provider` uses **inherited widgets** to propagate state down the widget tree and rebuild parts of the UI when state changes.

- **How it works**:
    - ○ `ChangeNotifierProvider`: This widget listens to a `ChangeNotifier` (which holds the state) and rebuilds the UI when the state changes.

111

- o Consumer: A widget that rebuilds whenever the ChangeNotifier it's listening to updates its state.
- **Basic Example with Provider**:

```dart

class Counter extends ChangeNotifier {
  int _count = 0;

  int get count => _count;

  void increment() {
    _count++;
    notifyListeners();  // Notifies all
listeners (UI widgets) to rebuild.
  }
}

void main() {
  runApp(
    ChangeNotifierProvider(
      create: (context) => Counter(),
      child: MyApp(),
    ),
  );
}

class MyApp extends StatelessWidget {
```

```
@override
Widget build(BuildContext context) {
  return MaterialApp(
    home: Scaffold(
      appBar:                AppBar(title:
Text('Provider Example')),
        body: Center(
          child: Consumer<Counter>(
            builder:  (context,  counter,
child) {
              return          Text('Count:
${counter.count}');
            },
          ),
        ),
        floatingActionButton:
FloatingActionButton(
          onPressed:        ()          =>
context.read<Counter>().increment(),
          child: Icon(Icons.add),
        ),
      ),
    );
  }
}
```

In this example, the Counter class extends ChangeNotifier and notifies the UI to update when the count changes. ChangeNotifierProvider is used to provide the Counter object to the widget tree, and `Consumer` is used to rebuild the widget when the count changes.

---

2. Riverpod

`Riverpod` is a newer and more advanced state management solution for Flutter, developed by the creator of `Provider`. It is a more flexible and robust alternative to `Provider` that allows for better separation of concerns, testability, and support for more complex use cases.

- **How it works**:
  - o Riverpod provides a `Provider` (similar to `ChangeNotifierProvider`) but with greater control over how and when the state is created, shared, and disposed of.
- **Basic Example with Riverpod**:

```dart

final            counterProvider         =
StateProvider((ref) => 0);

void main() {
  runApp(
    ProviderScope(
```

```dart
      child: MyApp(),
    ),
  );
}

class MyApp extends ConsumerWidget {
  @override
  Widget    build(BuildContext    context,
ScopedReader watch) {
    final           count           =
watch(counterProvider).state;

    return MaterialApp(
      home: Scaffold(
        appBar:              AppBar(title:
Text('Riverpod Example')),
        body:  Center(child:  Text('Count:
$count')),
        floatingActionButton:
FloatingActionButton(
          onPressed:         ()          =>
context.read(counterProvider).state++,
          child: Icon(Icons.add),
        ),
      ),
    );
  }
}
```

In this example, we use `StateProvider` to create a simple counter and use `ConsumerWidget` to listen for changes in the state. `Riverpod` is more powerful for handling more complex state management scenarios and is preferred in large-scale applications.

---

3. BLoC (Business Logic Component)

The BLoC pattern is a more structured and scalable way of managing state, especially for larger and more complex apps. BLoC relies on the concept of streams and sinks, where the business logic is separated from the UI. It uses **Streams** to manage state and event handling, making it ideal for applications that involve complex asynchronous data flows.

- **How it works**:
    - Events are added to a `Stream` (sinks).
    - The `BLoC` reacts to events by emitting new states through a stream.
    - The UI listens to the stream and updates when the state changes.
- **Basic Example with BLoC**:

```dart
class CounterBloc {
```

```
  final     _counterStateController     =
StreamController<int>.broadcast();
  StreamSink<int>    get    _inCounter   =>
_counterStateController.sink;
  Stream<int>        get    counter      =>
_counterStateController.stream;

  int _counter = 0;

  void increment() {
    _counter++;
    _inCounter.add(_counter);  // Emit the
new state.
  }

  void dispose() {
    _counterStateController.close();
  }
}

void main() {
  final counterBloc = CounterBloc();

  runApp(
    MaterialApp(
      home: Scaffold(
        appBar: AppBar(title: Text('BLoC
Example')),
        body: Center(
```

```
                child: StreamBuilder<int>(
                    stream: counterBloc.counter,
                    builder: (context, snapshot) {
                        return              Text('Count:
${snapshot.data ?? 0}');
                        },
                    ),
                ),
                floatingActionButton:
FloatingActionButton(
                    onPressed:           ()              =>
counterBloc.increment(),
                    child: Icon(Icons.add),
                ),
            ),
        ),
    );
}
```

In this example, the `CounterBloc` class handles the state of the counter and uses streams to emit updated state values. The `StreamBuilder` listens for updates and rebuilds the widget when a new count is emitted.

---

4. Redux

Redux is another popular state management technique, primarily used in large-scale applications with complex state. It is based on a unidirectional data flow pattern and involves three core principles: **actions**, **reducers**, and **stores**.

- **How it works**:
  - **Actions**: Events that describe what happened in the app (e.g., increment).
  - **Reducers**: Functions that specify how the state changes in response to an action.
  - **Store**: The single source of truth for the app's state.
- **Basic Example with Redux**:

```dart

class AppState {
  final int count;
  AppState({required this.count});
}

AppState counterReducer(AppState state,
dynamic action) {
  if (action == 'increment') {
    return AppState(count: state.count +
1);
  }
  return state;
```

```
}

final                    store                =
Store<AppState>(counterReducer,
initialState: AppState(count: 0));

void main() {
  runApp(MyApp());
}

class MyApp extends StatelessWidget {
  @override
  Widget build(BuildContext context) {
    return MaterialApp(
      home: Scaffold(
        appBar: AppBar(title: Text('Redux
Example')),
        body: Center(
          child: StoreConnector<AppState,
int>(
            converter:      (store)        =>
store.state.count,
            builder: (context, count) {
              return           Text('Count:
$count');
            },
          ),
        ),
```

```
        floatingActionButton:
FloatingActionButton(
            onPressed:          ()              =>
store.dispatch('increment'),
            child: Icon(Icons.add),
          ),
        ),
      );
    }
  }
```

In this example, we use Redux to manage the state of the counter. The Store holds the application state, and the StoreConnector widget listens for state changes and rebuilds the UI accordingly.

Practical Example of State Management in a To-Do List App

Let's implement a simple **to-do list** app using Provider, one of the easiest state management solutions. In this app, we will add tasks to a list, mark them as done, and remove them.

1. Model for To-Do Item:

```dart

class Todo {
  String title;
  bool isDone;
```

```dart
Todo({
    required this.title,
    this.isDone = false,
  });
}
```

2. To-Do List State (ChangeNotifier):

```
dart
```

```dart
class TodoListProvider extends ChangeNotifier {
  List<Todo> _todos = [];

  List<Todo> get todos => _todos;

  void addTask(String task) {
    _todos.add(Todo(title: task));
    notifyListeners();
  }

  void toggleTaskStatus(int index) {
    _todos[index].isDone                       =
!_todos[index].isDone;
    notifyListeners();
  }

  void removeTask(int index) {
    _todos.removeAt(index);
    notifyListeners();
```

```dart
    }
}
```

3. Main App and UI:

```
dart
```

```dart
void main() {
  runApp(
    ChangeNotifierProvider(
      create: (context) => TodoListProvider(),
      child: MyApp(),
    ),
  );
}

class MyApp extends StatelessWidget {
  @override
  Widget build(BuildContext context) {
    return MaterialApp(
      home: TodoListScreen(),
    );
  }
}

class TodoListScreen extends StatelessWidget {
  @override
  Widget build(BuildContext context) {
    final            todoProvider            =
Provider.of<TodoListProvider>(context);
```

123

```
    return Scaffold(
      appBar: AppBar(title: Text('To-Do List')),
      body: ListView.builder(
        itemCount: todoProvider.todos.length,
        itemBuilder: (context, index) {
          final              todo              =
todoProvider.todos[index];
          return ListTile(
            title: Text(todo.title),
            leading: Checkbox(
              value: todo.isDone,
              onChanged:          (_)           =>
todoProvider.toggleTaskStatus(index),
            ),
            trailing: IconButton(
              icon: Icon(Icons.delete),
              onPressed:          ()            =>
todoProvider.removeTask(index),
            ),
          );
        },
      ),
      floatingActionButton:
FloatingActionButton(
        onPressed:             ()             =>
todoProvider.addTask('New Task'),
        child: Icon(Icons.add),
      ),
```

```
    );
  }
}
```

In this example:

- We define a `Todo` model with a title and completion status (`isDone`).
- The `TodoListProvider` class extends `ChangeNotifier` to manage the state of the to-do list. It provides methods to add, remove, and toggle the status of tasks.
- The `TodoListScreen` listens to the `TodoListProvider` and updates the UI based on state changes.

Conclusion

State management in Flutter is a critical skill for building scalable and maintainable apps. Whether you use simple solutions like **Provider** or **Riverpod**, or more complex patterns like **BLoC** and **Redux**, each technique has its strengths and fits different app needs. In this chapter, we've covered how to manage state effectively, from basic examples to complex applications like a to-do list.

By understanding and applying the appropriate state management technique, you can build apps that are easier to maintain and scale as your app grows in complexity.

CHAPTER 11

HANDLING USER INPUT AND FORMS

Handling User Input in Flutter

In Flutter, handling user input is a key part of creating interactive applications. Flutter provides a wide variety of widgets to capture user input, including text fields, checkboxes, and radio buttons. Each of these widgets allows you to collect data from users in different ways.

1. TextInput

The `TextField` widget is used to collect text input from users. It is one of the most common input widgets in Flutter, and it allows you to customize the appearance and behavior of the input field.

- **Basic Example**:

```dart
TextField(
```

```
decoration: InputDecoration(
  labelText: 'Enter your name',
),
onChanged: (text) {
  print("User input: $text");
},
);
```

- **Key Properties**:
  - `decoration`: Used to style the input field, such as adding labels, hint text, or icons.
  - `onChanged`: A callback that is triggered whenever the user changes the input.

2. TextInput with Controller

To retrieve and manipulate the text entered by the user, you can use a `TextEditingController`.

- **Example with Controller**:

```dart

TextEditingController    _controller    =
TextEditingController();

@override
Widget build(BuildContext context) {
  return TextField(
```

```
        controller: _controller,
        decoration: InputDecoration(labelText:
'Enter your name'),
    );
}


void getInput() {
    String userInput = _controller.text;
    print("User input: $userInput");
}
```

In this example, _controller holds the value entered in the TextField, which can be retrieved using _controller.text.

---

3. Checkboxes

Checkboxes allow users to select or deselect an option. The Checkbox widget in Flutter is used for this purpose.

- **Basic Example**:

```dart
bool isChecked = false;

Checkbox(
  value: isChecked,
  onChanged: (bool? value) {
```

```
    setState(() {
      isChecked = value!;
    });
  },
);
```

- **Key Properties**:
  - o value: The current state of the checkbox (true for checked, false for unchecked).
  - o onChanged: A callback that is triggered when the checkbox is tapped. The new state is passed as an argument.

---

4. Radio Buttons

Radio buttons are used when you want to allow the user to choose one option from a set. Flutter uses the Radio widget for this purpose.

- **Basic Example**:

```
dart

int? selectedValue = 1;

Row(
  children: <Widget>[
```

```
Radio<int>(
  value: 1,
  groupValue: selectedValue,
  onChanged: (int? value) {
    setState(() {
      selectedValue = value;
    });
  },
),
Text('Option 1'),
Radio<int>(
  value: 2,
  groupValue: selectedValue,
  onChanged: (int? value) {
    setState(() {
      selectedValue = value;
    });
  },
),
Text('Option 2'),
  ],
);
```

- **Key Properties**:
  - o `value`: The value of the radio button.
  - o `groupValue`: The current value of the selected radio button in the group.

o   `onChanged`: A callback function that updates the `groupValue` when the user selects a radio button.

Validating Forms

Form validation ensures that the data entered by the user is correct and complete before submitting the form. Flutter provides the `Form` widget and `TextFormField` widget for handling form input and validation.

---

1. Creating a Form

A `Form` widget holds multiple form fields, such as `TextFormField` widgets, and provides validation logic for them. To manage the state of the form, Flutter uses a `GlobalKey<FormState>`.

- **Basic Form Example**:

```dart
final _formKey = GlobalKey<FormState>();

@override
```

```
Widget build(BuildContext context) {
  return Scaffold(
    appBar:   AppBar(title:    Text('Form
Validation')),
    body: Padding(
      padding: EdgeInsets.all(16.0),
      child: Form(
        key: _formKey,
        child: Column(
          children: <Widget>[
            TextFormField(
              decoration:
InputDecoration(labelText: 'Username'),
              validator: (value) {
                if (value == null ||
value.isEmpty) {
                  return 'Please enter a
username';
                }
                return null;
              },
            ),
            TextFormField(
              decoration:
InputDecoration(labelText: 'Password'),
              obscureText: true,
              validator: (value) {
                if (value == null ||
value.isEmpty) {
```

133

```
                    return 'Please enter a
password';
                }
                return null;
            },
          ),
          ElevatedButton(
            onPressed: () {
              if
(_formKey.currentState!.validate()) {
                  // Form is valid,
perform login or other actions
                  print('Form submitted');
                }
            },
            child: Text('Submit'),
          ),
        ],
      ),
    ),
  ),
);
}
```

- **Key Concepts**:
  - `GlobalKey<FormState>`: Used to manage the form's state, including validation and submission.

134

- TextFormField: A form field widget that is integrated with the Form widget and supports validation.
- validator: A function that checks the validity of the input field and returns an error message if the input is invalid.

2. Common Validation Scenarios

- **Required Fields**: Ensure that the user enters data in the field.

```dart
String? validateRequired(String? value) {
  if (value == null || value.isEmpty) {
    return 'This field is required';
  }
  return null;
}
```

- **Email Validation**: Use a regular expression to validate email format.

```dart
String? validateEmail(String? value) {
```

```
final regex = RegExp(r'^[a-zA-Z0-9]+@[a-
zA-Z0-9]+\.[a-zA-Z]+');
  if (value == null || value.isEmpty) {
    return 'Please enter an email';
  } else if (!regex.hasMatch(value)) {
    return 'Please enter a valid email';
  }
  return null;
}
```

Implementing a Login Screen with Form Validation

Let's now build a login screen with a form that validates the username and password input. This screen will use the `Form` and `TextFormField` widgets to collect the user's credentials and ensure the data is valid before submitting.

1. Login Screen Example:

dart

```
class LoginScreen extends StatefulWidget {
  @override
  _LoginScreenState       createState()        =>
_LoginScreenState();
}
```

```
class           _LoginScreenState           extends
State<LoginScreen> {
  final _formKey = GlobalKey<FormState>();
  final             _usernameController           =
TextEditingController();
  final             _passwordController           =
TextEditingController();

  @override
  Widget build(BuildContext context) {
    return Scaffold(
      appBar: AppBar(title: Text('Login')),
      body: Padding(
        padding: EdgeInsets.all(16.0),
        child: Form(
          key: _formKey,
          child: Column(
            children: <Widget>[
              TextFormField(
                controller: _usernameController,
                decoration:
InputDecoration(labelText: 'Username'),
                validator: (value) {
                  if  (value  ==  null  ||
value.isEmpty) {
                    return  'Please  enter  a
username';
                  }
                  return null;
```

137

```
              },
            ),
          TextFormField(
            controller: _passwordController,
            decoration:
InputDecoration(labelText: 'Password'),
            obscureText: true,
            validator: (value) {
              if    (value    ==    null    ||
value.isEmpty) {
                return    'Please    enter    a
password';
              } else if (value.length < 6) {
                return 'Password must be at
least 6 characters';
              }
              return null;
            },
          ),
          ElevatedButton(
            onPressed: () {
              if
(_formKey.currentState!.validate()) {
                // Handle login logic here
                print('Username:
${_usernameController.text}');
                print('Password:
${_passwordController.text}');
              }
```

```
                },
                child: Text('Login'),
            ),
        ],
      ),
    ),
  ),
);
}
}
```

- **Explanation**:
    - TextEditingController: Manages the text input by the user for both the username and password fields.
    - validator: Validates the inputs for both username and password. If validation fails, it shows an error message.
    - obscureText: Ensures that the password is hidden as the user types.
    - The ElevatedButton triggers the form submission, where we check if the form is valid using
      _formKey.currentState!.validate().

Conclusion

Handling user input and forms is a crucial aspect of building interactive apps in Flutter. By using widgets like `TextField`, `Checkbox`, and `Radio`, you can easily collect input from users. Flutter's `Form` and `TextFormField` widgets provide a powerful way to handle form validation and ensure that the data entered by the user is correct before submitting. Implementing form validation enhances the user experience by providing immediate feedback when invalid data is entered.

With the knowledge of how to handle input and validate forms in Flutter, you can create robust, user-friendly forms for any app.

CHAPTER 12

WORKING WITH APIS IN FLUTTER

Introduction to HTTP Requests

In modern mobile applications, communicating with remote servers or APIs (Application Programming Interfaces) is essential for fetching and sending data. Flutter provides the `http` package for making HTTP requests, enabling you to interact with RESTful services, fetch data from web servers, and more.

The `http` package allows you to send HTTP requests like GET, POST, PUT, and DELETE. These requests allow your app to retrieve data from a server, send data to the server, or perform other actions.

---

1. Setting up the HTTP package

To get started with making HTTP requests in Flutter, you'll need to add the `http` package to your project.

1. **Add the http package** to your `pubspec.yaml` file:

```yaml
yaml

dependencies:
  flutter:
    sdk: flutter
  http: ^0.13.3
```

2. **Run** `flutter pub get` to install the package.

---

2. Making a Basic HTTP Request

The most common type of request is the `GET` request, which retrieves data from a remote server. Here's how you can use the `http` package to make a basic HTTP request.

- **Example of a GET request**:

```dart
dart

import 'package:http/http.dart' as http;

Future<void> fetchData() async {
  final       response       =       await
http.get(Uri.parse('https://jsonplacehold
er.typicode.com/posts'));

  if (response.statusCode == 200) {
```

```
    // If the server returns a successful
response
    print('Data fetched successfully');
    print(response.body); // Prints the
raw response body
  } else {
    // If the server returns an error
    print('Failed to load data');
  }
}
```

In the example above:

- `http.get`: Makes a `GET` request to the provided URL.
- `await`: Waits for the response asynchronously.
- `response.statusCode`: Checks if the request was successful (HTTP status code 200).
- `response.body`: Contains the raw response data, typically in JSON format.

Parsing JSON Data

In most cases, the data retrieved from APIs is in JSON format. Flutter has built-in support for parsing JSON using the `dart:convert` package.

To parse JSON data, you'll typically:

1. Retrieve the JSON data from the response body.

2. Convert it into a Dart object (usually a `Map<String, dynamic>` or a list of objects).

3. Map the data into model classes for easier manipulation.

---

1. Parsing JSON with `dart:convert`

You can use the `jsonDecode` function from the `dart:convert` package to convert a JSON string into a Dart object.

- **Example of parsing JSON**:

```dart

import 'dart:convert';

// Example response body (JSON string)
String responseBody = '''
[
  {"userId": 1, "id": 1, "title": "First Post", "body": "This is the first post."},
  {"userId": 1, "id": 2, "title": "Second Post", "body": "This is the second post."}
]
''';

// Parsing JSON
```

```
List<dynamic>          parsedData          =
jsonDecode(responseBody);
print(parsedData); // Prints the decoded
JSON

// Converting to a list of models
List<Post> posts = parsedData.map((data)
=> Post.fromJson(data)).toList();
```

- **Defining a Model Class for Posts**:

```dart
dart

class Post {
  final int userId;
  final int id;
  final String title;
  final String body;

  Post({required this.userId, required
this.id, required this.title, required
this.body});

  // Factory constructor for creating a
Post from JSON data
  factory     Post.fromJson(Map<String,
dynamic> json) {
    return Post(
      userId: json['userId'],
      id: json['id'],
```

145

```
      title: json['title'],
      body: json['body'],
    );
  }
}
```

In this example:

- The jsonDecode function converts a JSON string into a Dart object.
- The Post model class is used to map the data into a structured format.
- The fromJson factory constructor allows us to easily convert a JSON map into an instance of the Post model.

---

2. Fetching and Parsing JSON from an API

Now let's combine the API request and JSON parsing to fetch data from an API and display it in a structured format.

- **Complete Example of Fetching and Parsing JSON:**

  dart

  ```dart
  import 'package:http/http.dart' as http;
  import 'dart:convert';
  ```

146

```dart
class Post {
  final int userId;
  final int id;
  final String title;
  final String body;

  Post({required this.userId, required
this.id, required this.title, required
this.body});

  factory         Post.fromJson(Map<String,
dynamic> json) {
    return Post(
      userId: json['userId'],
      id: json['id'],
      title: json['title'],
      body: json['body'],
    );
  }
}

Future<List<Post>> fetchPosts() async {
  final         response         =         await
http.get(Uri.parse('https://jsonplacehold
er.typicode.com/posts'));

  if (response.statusCode == 200) {
    List<dynamic>         data         =
jsonDecode(response.body);
```

```
    return        data.map((item)        =>
Post.fromJson(item)).toList();
  } else {
    throw    Exception('Failed   to   load
posts');
  }
}
```

- **Explanation**:
  - We fetch the posts using the `http.get` method.
  - We parse the response body (JSON) using `jsonDecode` and convert it into a list of `Post` objects using the `Post.fromJson` constructor.
  - If the API call is successful (status code 200), we return the parsed list; otherwise, we throw an error.

Displaying API Data in Flutter Widgets

Once you've fetched and parsed data from the API, you need to display it in the app's UI. You can use Flutter's widgets such as `ListView` to display a dynamic list of data.

---

1. Displaying Data with `ListView`

You can use `ListView.builder` to display a list of items dynamically in your app. This is efficient because it only builds the items that are visible on the screen, saving memory and improving performance.

- **Example of Displaying Posts in a List**:

```dart
class PostsScreen extends StatefulWidget {
  @override
  _PostsScreenState    createState()    =>
_PostsScreenState();
}

class    _PostsScreenState    extends
State<PostsScreen> {
  late Future<List<Post>> futurePosts;

  @override
  void initState() {
    super.initState();
    futurePosts = fetchPosts();
  }

  @override
  Widget build(BuildContext context) {
    return Scaffold(
```

```
        appBar:                    AppBar(title:
Text('Posts')),
        body: FutureBuilder<List<Post>>(
          future: futurePosts,
          builder: (context, snapshot) {
            if (snapshot.connectionState ==
ConnectionState.waiting) {
              return            Center(child:
CircularProgressIndicator());
            } else if (snapshot.hasError) {
              return            Center(child:
Text('Error: ${snapshot.error}'));
            } else if (!snapshot.hasData ||
snapshot.data!.isEmpty) {
              return Center(child: Text('No
posts available.'));
            } else {
              final posts = snapshot.data!;
              return ListView.builder(
                itemCount: posts.length,
                itemBuilder:         (context,
index) {
                  return ListTile(
                    title:
Text(posts[index].title),
                    subtitle:
Text(posts[index].body),
                  );
                },
```

```
        );
      }
    },
  ),
);
}
}
```

- **Explanation**:
  - We use `FutureBuilder` to handle the asynchronous nature of fetching data.
  - The `FutureBuilder` listens for the completion of the `fetchPosts()` function and updates the UI accordingly.
  - When the data is loaded, we display it in a `ListView.builder`, where each item is displayed using a `ListTile`.

2. Handling Errors and Loading States

The `FutureBuilder` widget is ideal for handling the loading and error states when fetching data asynchronously.

- **Loading State**: While the data is being fetched, we display a `CircularProgressIndicator`.

- **Error State**: If the request fails, we display an error message.
- **Empty Data State**: If no data is returned, we show a message indicating that no posts are available.

Conclusion

Working with APIs in Flutter is a fundamental skill for building data-driven apps. By using the `http` package, you can easily send HTTP requests, parse the JSON responses, and display the data in your app using Flutter's widgets. The combination of **FutureBuilder** for asynchronous operations and **ListView.builder** for displaying dynamic lists makes handling API data in Flutter both efficient and straightforward.

As you continue working with APIs, you'll encounter more complex use cases like authentication, paginated data, and caching, but this chapter provides a solid foundation to get started with fetching and displaying data in Flutter apps.

CHAPTER 13

LOCAL DATA STORAGE WITH SQLITE AND SHAREDPREFERENCES

Storing Data Locally Using SQLite

When building mobile apps, it's often necessary to store data locally on the device, especially for apps that need to function offline or store user settings. Flutter provides several options for local data storage, two of the most common being **SQLite** and **SharedPreferences**. SQLite is ideal for structured data and complex queries, while SharedPreferences is perfect for simple key-value data.

In this section, we'll explore how to use **SQLite** to store structured data in Flutter.

1. Setting Up SQLite in Flutter

To use SQLite in Flutter, you'll need to use the `sqflite` package. This package provides an interface for interacting with SQLite databases on both Android and iOS.

Step 1: Add the `sqflite` package

First, add `sqflite` to your `pubspec.yaml` file:

yaml

```
dependencies:
  flutter:
    sdk: flutter
  sqflite: ^2.0.0+3
  path: ^1.8.0  # For handling file paths
```

Run `flutter pub get` to install the dependencies.

---

2. Creating a Database

SQLite works by creating a database on the device's file system. You can store multiple tables and use SQL queries to interact with the data.

Here's an example of how to create a database and store data in it.

Step 2: Create a Database Helper Class

154

```dart
dart

import 'package:sqflite/sqflite.dart';
import 'package:path/path.dart';

class DatabaseHelper {
  static final DatabaseHelper instance = DatabaseHelper._init();
  static Database? _database;

  DatabaseHelper._init();

  Future<Database> get database async {
    if (_database != null) return _database!;
    _database = await _initDB('my_database.db');
    return _database!;
  }

  Future<Database> _initDB(String path) async {
    final dbPath = await getDatabasesPath();
    final dbLocation = join(dbPath, path);
    return await openDatabase(dbLocation, version: 1, onCreate: _createDB);
  }

  Future _createDB(Database db, int version) async {
    const idType = 'INTEGER PRIMARY KEY AUTOINCREMENT';
```

155

```
    const textType = 'TEXT NOT NULL';
    await db.execute('''CREATE TABLE users (
        id $idType,
        name $textType,
        email $textType
    )''');
  }


  Future<int> addUser(Map<String, dynamic> user)
async {
    final db = await instance.database;
    return await db.insert('users', user);
  }


  Future<List<Map<String, dynamic>>> getUsers()
async {
    final db = await instance.database;
    return await db.query('users');
  }
}
```

In the `DatabaseHelper` class:

- **`_initDB`** initializes the database.
- **`_createDB`** creates a `users` table with `id`, `name`, and `email` fields.
- **`addUser`** inserts a new user into the database.
- **`getUsers`** retrieves all users from the `users` table.

3. Using the Database Helper

To interact with the SQLite database, you can call the methods of the `DatabaseHelper` class.

Step 3: Using the Database in Your App

```dart
class MyHomePage extends StatefulWidget {
  @override
  _MyHomePageState          createState()           =>
_MyHomePageState();
}

class _MyHomePageState extends State<MyHomePage>
{
  final TextEditingController _nameController =
TextEditingController();
  final TextEditingController _emailController =
TextEditingController();

  void _addUser() async {
    final user = {
      'name': _nameController.text,
      'email': _emailController.text,
    };
    await DatabaseHelper.instance.addUser(user);
```

```
   setState(() {});
 }


 Future<List<Map<String, dynamic>>> _getUsers()
async {
   return                              await
DatabaseHelper.instance.getUsers();
 }


 @override
 Widget build(BuildContext context) {
   return Scaffold(
     appBar:    AppBar(title:    Text('SQLite
Example')),
     body: Column(
       children: [
         TextField(controller: _nameController,
decoration: InputDecoration(labelText: 'Name')),
         TextField(controller:
_emailController,                    decoration:
InputDecoration(labelText: 'Email')),
         ElevatedButton(onPressed:    _addUser,
child: Text('Add User')),
         Expanded(
           child:
FutureBuilder<List<Map<String, dynamic>>>(
             future: _getUsers(),
             builder: (context, snapshot) {
```

```
                    if (snapshot.connectionState ==
ConnectionState.waiting) {
                    return          Center(child:
CircularProgressIndicator());
                    }
                    if (snapshot.hasError) {
                    return          Center(child:
Text('Error: ${snapshot.error}'));
                    }
                    final users = snapshot.data ??
[];
                    return ListView.builder(
                       itemCount: users.length,
                       itemBuilder: (context, index)
{
                          return ListTile(
                             title:
Text(users[index]['name']),
                             subtitle:
Text(users[index]['email']),
                          );
                       },
                    );
                 },
               ),
             ),
          ],
        ),
      );
```

```
  }
}
```

In this example:

- The `TextField` widgets capture user input for the name and email.
- When the "Add User" button is pressed, the data is stored in SQLite using the `addUser` method from the `DatabaseHelper` class.
- The `FutureBuilder` widget is used to display the list of users fetched from the database.

Using SharedPreferences for Simple Key-Value Storage

For simpler data storage, where you don't need complex queries or structured tables, **SharedPreferences** is a great option. It allows you to store small amounts of data as key-value pairs, such as settings, flags, or user preferences.

---

1. Setting Up SharedPreferences

First, add the `shared_preferences` package to your `pubspec.yaml`:

```yaml
yaml

dependencies:
  shared_preferences: ^2.0.7
```

Then run `flutter pub get` to install the package.

---

2. Using SharedPreferences

SharedPreferences is typically used for storing simple types like `String`, `int`, `double`, `bool`, and `List<String>`.

- **Basic Example of Using SharedPreferences**:

```dart
dart

import
'package:shared_preferences/shared_prefer
ences.dart';

Future<void> saveData() async {
  SharedPreferences    prefs    =    await
SharedPreferences.getInstance();
  await        prefs.setString('username',
'john_doe');
  await prefs.setInt('age', 30);
}
```

```dart
Future<void> loadData() async {
  SharedPreferences prefs = await
SharedPreferences.getInstance();
  String? username =
prefs.getString('username');
  int? age = prefs.getInt('age');
  print('Username: $username, Age: $age');
}
```

In this example:

- **setString** and **setInt** are used to store a string and an integer.
- **getString** and **getInt** are used to retrieve the values from SharedPreferences.

---

3. Practical Example of Using SharedPreferences

Here's how you can use SharedPreferences to store user preferences such as a theme choice (light or dark mode):

dart

```dart
class PreferencesService {
  Future<void> saveThemePreference(bool
isDarkMode) async {
```

```
    SharedPreferences       prefs     =       await
SharedPreferences.getInstance();
    await                prefs.setBool('isDarkMode',
isDarkMode);
  }

  Future<bool> getThemePreference() async {
    SharedPreferences       prefs     =       await
SharedPreferences.getInstance();
    return prefs.getBool('isDarkMode') ?? false;
// Default to light mode
  }
}
```

You can call these methods to save and retrieve the theme preference throughout your app.

Practical Examples of Data Storage

Let's now combine both SQLite and SharedPreferences into a single Flutter app to demonstrate how you can use them together for different types of data storage.

---

1. Example: Storing Settings in SharedPreferences and User Data in SQLite

163

```dart
dart

class SettingsScreen extends StatefulWidget {
  @override
  _SettingsScreenState createState() =>
_SettingsScreenState();
}

class _SettingsScreenState extends
State<SettingsScreen> {
  final PreferencesService _preferencesService =
PreferencesService();
  bool _isDarkMode = false;

  @override
  void initState() {
    super.initState();
    _loadSettings();
  }

  _loadSettings() async {
    bool darkMode = await
_preferencesService.getThemePreference();
    setState(() {
      _isDarkMode = darkMode;
    });
  }

  _toggleDarkMode() async {
```

```
    setState(() {
      _isDarkMode = !_isDarkMode;
    });
    await
_preferencesService.saveThemePreference(_isDark
Mode);
  }

  @override
  Widget build(BuildContext context) {
    return Scaffold(
      appBar: AppBar(title: Text('Settings')),
      body: SwitchListTile(
        title: Text('Dark Mode'),
        value: _isDarkMode,
        onChanged: (bool value) {
          _toggleDarkMode();
        },
      ),
    );
  }
}
```

In this example:

- **SharedPreferences** is used to store and retrieve the user's theme preference.
- The switch in the UI lets the user toggle between light and dark modes, and the state is saved in SharedPreferences.

165

Conclusion

Local data storage is crucial in mobile app development, and Flutter provides powerful solutions such as **SQLite** and **SharedPreferences** for different storage needs:

- **SQLite** is perfect for storing structured data with complex queries and relationships.
- **SharedPreferences** is ideal for simple key-value pairs, like settings or flags.

By understanding how to use both SQLite and SharedPreferences effectively, you can manage data locally in your Flutter app and provide a seamless experience for users, even when they are offline.

CHAPTER 14

FLUTTER ANIMATIONS

Basics of Flutter Animations

Animations play a crucial role in creating dynamic and engaging user experiences. In Flutter, animations are used to enhance the user interface (UI) by smoothly transitioning between different visual states, making your app feel more responsive and interactive. Flutter provides a rich set of animation classes and tools to make adding animations to your app both straightforward and powerful.

Animations in Flutter are based on the **Animation** class and the **AnimationController** class. These classes allow you to define how a widget's properties change over time. An animation consists of:

- **Animation value**: The value that changes over time.
- **AnimationController**: The controller that manages the animation's duration, curve, and other properties.

1. Basic Animation Structure:

To create an animation in Flutter, you typically:

- Define an `AnimationController` that governs the duration and behavior of the animation.
- Use an `Animation` object to define the value changes over time (e.g., changing the position, size, or color of a widget).
- Use a `TickerProvider` (like `SingleTickerProviderStateMixin`) to provide a ticking clock for the animation.

Example of a basic animation setup:

dart

```dart
class MyAnimatedWidget extends StatefulWidget {
  @override
  _MyAnimatedWidgetState    createState()    =>
_MyAnimatedWidgetState();
}

class      _MyAnimatedWidgetState      extends
State<MyAnimatedWidget>                   with
SingleTickerProviderStateMixin {
  late AnimationController _controller;
  late Animation<double> _animation;
```

168

```
@override
void initState() {
  super.initState();
  _controller = AnimationController(
    duration: Duration(seconds: 2),
    vsync: this, // Provides the ticker
  );

  _animation = Tween<double>(begin: 0.0, end:
300.0).animate(CurvedAnimation(
    parent: _controller,
    curve: Curves.easeInOut,
  ));

  _controller.repeat(reverse:      true);      //
Repeats animation and reverses after reaching end
}

@override
Widget build(BuildContext context) {
  return Scaffold(
    appBar:      AppBar(title:      Text('Basic
Animation')),
    body: Center(
      child: AnimatedBuilder(
        animation: _animation,
        builder: (context, child) {
          return Container(
            width: _animation.value,
```

```
            height: _animation.value,
            color: Colors.blue,
          );
        },
      ),
    ),
  );
}


@override
void dispose() {
  _controller.dispose();   // Clean  up  the
controller when the widget is disposed
   super.dispose();
  }
}
```

In this example:

- **AnimationController**: Controls the animation's duration and synchronization.
- **Tween**: Specifies the start (`begin`) and end (`end`) values for the animation (in this case, a size change).
- **CurvedAnimation**: Applies a curve to the animation, making it more natural.
- **AnimatedBuilder**: A widget that listens to the animation and rebuilds parts of the widget tree based on the animation's progress.

Implicit and Explicit Animations

Flutter provides two types of animations:

- **Implicit Animations**: These animations are built into specific widgets in Flutter and automatically handle the animation for you.
- **Explicit Animations**: These require manual setup with `AnimationController` and `Tween` to create custom animations.

1. Implicit Animations

Implicit animations are the easiest to implement in Flutter. You simply need to wrap a widget with an animation widget, and Flutter takes care of animating the changes for you. Examples of implicit animations include `AnimatedContainer`, `AnimatedOpacity`, `AnimatedPositioned`, and `AnimatedSwitcher`.

- **Example of Implicit Animation (AnimatedContainer)**:

```dart
dart

class AnimatedBox extends StatefulWidget {
```

```
@override
_AnimatedBoxState    createState()    =>
_AnimatedBoxState();
}


class       _AnimatedBoxState       extends
State<AnimatedBox> {
  double _width = 100;
  double _height = 100;

  void _animateBox() {
    setState(() {
      _width = _width == 100 ? 200 : 100;
      _height = _height == 100 ? 200 : 100;
    });
  }

  @override
  Widget build(BuildContext context) {
    return Scaffold(
      appBar: AppBar(title: Text('Implicit
Animation')),
      body: Center(
        child: GestureDetector(
          onTap: _animateBox,
          child: AnimatedContainer(
            duration:    Duration(seconds:
1),
              width: _width,
```

```
            height: _height,
            color: Colors.blue,
            curve: Curves.easeInOut,
          ),
        ),
      ),
    );
  }
}
```

In this example:

- `AnimatedContainer`: This widget automatically animates changes to its properties (like `width`, `height`, and `color`).
- `duration`: Specifies the duration of the animation.
- `curve`: Defines the easing curve for the animation.

Implicit animations are great for simple changes like size, color, and opacity without needing a lot of custom code.

2. Explicit Animations

Explicit animations give you more control over how the animation behaves and what properties change. These animations involve using `AnimationController`, `Tween`, and `AnimatedBuilder`.

173

- **Example of Explicit Animation (Custom Animation with AnimationController)**:

dart

```
class        MyCustomAnimation        extends
StatefulWidget {
  @override
  _MyCustomAnimationState createState() =>
_MyCustomAnimationState();
}

class    _MyCustomAnimationState     extends
State<MyCustomAnimation>               with
SingleTickerProviderStateMixin {
  late AnimationController _controller;
  late Animation<double> _animation;

  @override
  void initState() {
    super.initState();
    _controller = AnimationController(
      duration: Duration(seconds: 2),
      vsync: this,
    );

    _animation = Tween<double>(begin: 0.0,
end: 300.0).animate(CurvedAnimation(
      parent: _controller,
```

```
        curve: Curves.easeInOut,
    ));

    _controller.forward(); // Starts the
animation
  }

  @override
  Widget build(BuildContext context) {
    return Scaffold(
      appBar: AppBar(title: Text('Explicit
Animation')),
      body: Center(
        child: AnimatedBuilder(
          animation: _animation,
          builder: (context, child) {
            return Container(
              width: _animation.value,
              height: _animation.value,
              color: Colors.blue,
            );
          },
        ),
      ),
    );
  }

  @override
  void dispose() {
```

175

```
        _controller.dispose();
        super.dispose();
    }
  }
```

In this example:

- `AnimationController`: Controls the animation's behavior (such as starting, stopping, and repeating).
- `Tween`: Defines the range of values for the animation.
- `CurvedAnimation`: Applies an easing curve to the animation for smoother transitions.

Explicit animations are suitable for more complex and custom animations, such as when you need to animate specific properties or trigger animations based on user interactions.

Creating Custom Animations with AnimationController

`AnimationController` is the heart of Flutter's explicit animation system. It allows you to control the animation's duration, start/stop behavior, and repetition. You can combine `AnimationController` with `Tween` to create custom animations for widgets.

1. Example of Custom Animation with AnimationController:

Let's create a custom animation where a widget moves from left to right across the screen.

```dart
class MovingBox extends StatefulWidget {
  @override
  _MovingBoxState          createState()              =>
_MovingBoxState();
}

class  _MovingBoxState  extends  State<MovingBox>
with SingleTickerProviderStateMixin {
  late AnimationController _controller;
  late Animation<double> _animation;

  @override
  void initState() {
    super.initState();
    _controller = AnimationController(
      duration: Duration(seconds: 3),
      vsync: this,
    );

    _animation = Tween<double>(begin: 0.0, end:
300.0).animate(
      CurvedAnimation(
```

```
      parent: _controller,
      curve: Curves.easeInOut,
    ),
  );


  _controller.repeat(reverse:      true);      //
Repeats the animation back and forth
  }


  @override
  Widget build(BuildContext context) {
    return Scaffold(
      appBar:     AppBar(title:     Text('Custom
Animation')),
      body: Center(
        child: AnimatedBuilder(
          animation: _animation,
          builder: (context, child) {
            return Transform.translate(
              offset:     Offset(_animation.value,
0),
              child: child,
            );
          },
          child: Container(
            width: 100,
            height: 100,
            color: Colors.blue,
          ),
```

```
        ),
      ),
    );
  }

  @override
  void dispose() {
    _controller.dispose();
    super.dispose();
  }
}
```

In this example:

- Tween: Defines a movement from 0.0 to 300.0.
- Transform.translate: Moves the widget based on the animation value.
- repeat(reverse: true): Makes the widget move back and forth between the two points.

Conclusion

Flutter provides a rich set of tools for animations, allowing you to create smooth, interactive user interfaces. By using implicit and explicit animations, you can easily add visual effects to your app. Implicit animations are simple to implement, while explicit animations give you more control over the animation process, such as controlling the animation's behavior and adding custom transitions.

AnimationController and **Tween** allow for creating powerful and flexible animations that can respond to user input or internal app changes.

Whether you're building a simple animation or a complex interactive experience, Flutter's animation framework provides everything you need to bring your UI to life.

CHAPTER 15

CUSTOMIZING UI ELEMENTS

Customizing Buttons, Text Fields, and Cards

In Flutter, customization of UI elements is essential to make the app feel unique and align with the app's branding. Flutter provides extensive customization options for widgets like buttons, text fields, and cards, allowing you to design visually appealing and user-friendly interfaces.

1. Customizing Buttons

Flutter provides several types of buttons, such as `ElevatedButton`, `TextButton`, and `OutlinedButton`. You can customize these buttons to change their shape, color, size, and more.

- **Basic Button Customization**:

```dart
ElevatedButton(
  onPressed: () {
```

```
      // Action on press
    },
    style: ButtonStyle(
      backgroundColor:
MaterialStateProperty.all(Colors.blue),
      shape:
MaterialStateProperty.all(RoundedRectangl
eBorder(
        borderRadius:
BorderRadius.circular(12),
      )),
      padding:
MaterialStateProperty.all(EdgeInsets.symm
etric(vertical: 16, horizontal: 32)),
    ),
    child:   Text('Custom   Button',   style:
TextStyle(fontSize:      18,      color:
Colors.white)),
  );
```

In this example:

- **backgroundColor**: Changes the button's background color.
- **shape**: Applies a rounded rectangle shape to the button.
- **padding**: Sets custom padding inside the button.
- **child**: Defines the button's content, which is a Text widget in this case.

You can apply similar customizations to other button types like `TextButton` and `OutlinedButton`.

---

2. Customizing Text Fields

Text fields are crucial for user input, and Flutter offers a high level of customization for these widgets. You can style the borders, colors, text styles, and even add custom icons inside the field.

- **Basic Customization of a `TextField`:**

```dart
TextField(
  decoration: InputDecoration(
    labelText: 'Enter your name',
    hintText: 'John Doe',
    border: OutlineInputBorder(
      borderRadius:
BorderRadius.circular(12),
      borderSide:        BorderSide(color:
Colors.blue, width: 2),
    ),
    focusedBorder: OutlineInputBorder(
      borderRadius:
BorderRadius.circular(12),
```

```
        borderSide:         BorderSide(color:
Colors.green, width: 2),
      ),
      suffixIcon: Icon(Icons.person),
    ),
  );
```

In this example:

- **labelText**: The label inside the `TextField` widget.
- **hintText**: Placeholder text that appears when the field is empty.
- **border**: Defines the appearance of the input field's border.
- **focusedBorder**: Changes the border color when the field is focused.
- **suffixIcon**: Adds an icon inside the `TextField` at the end (right side).

---

3. Customizing Cards

`Card` widgets are commonly used to display content in a visually distinct container. You can customize the `Card` widget's shape, elevation, color, and add padding or margin for better presentation.

184

- **Customizing a Card**:

dart

```dart
Card(
  shape: RoundedRectangleBorder(
    borderRadius:
BorderRadius.circular(12),
  ),
  elevation: 5,
  color: Colors.lightBlueAccent,
  child: Padding(
    padding: EdgeInsets.all(16),
    child: Column(
      children: <Widget>[
        Text('Title',                style:
TextStyle(fontSize:    20,     fontWeight:
FontWeight.bold)),
        SizedBox(height: 10),
        Text('This  is  a  customized  card
with some content inside it.'),
      ],
    ),
  ),
);
```

In this example:

- **shape**: Defines the rounded corners for the card.

- **elevation**: Adds shadow to the card, giving it a 3D effect.
- **color**: Sets the background color of the card.
- **child**: Contains the content of the card, such as text or images.

Using Custom Fonts and Themes

Fonts and themes are essential to make the app's UI consistent with the brand's identity. Flutter allows you to define custom fonts and themes globally to ensure a cohesive look throughout the app.

---

1. Adding Custom Fonts

To use custom fonts in your Flutter app, you first need to add them to the `pubspec.yaml` file and then reference them in your app's theme.

- **Step 1: Add Custom Fonts to `pubspec.yaml`:**

```yaml
flutter:
  fonts:
    - family: CustomFont
```

```
    fonts:
        -     asset:     fonts/CustomFont-
Regular.ttf
        - asset: fonts/CustomFont-Bold.ttf
          weight: 700
```

- **Step 2: Use the Custom Font in Text Style**:

```dart
Text(
  'Hello, Custom Font!',
  style: TextStyle(
    fontFamily: 'CustomFont',
    fontSize: 24,
  ),
);
```

- **Step 3: Apply Custom Font Globally via Theme**:

```dart
ThemeData(
  textTheme: TextTheme(
    bodyText1:      TextStyle(fontFamily:
'CustomFont', fontSize: 18),
    bodyText2:      TextStyle(fontFamily:
'CustomFont', fontSize: 16),
  ),
);
```

In this example, the `CustomFont` is loaded from the assets and applied to a `Text` widget, both individually and globally through the `ThemeData`.

---

2. Using Themes for Global Styling

Flutter allows you to define a global `Theme` to standardize the appearance of your app. You can specify global styles for widgets like text, buttons, icons, etc., using `ThemeData`.

- **Setting up a Global Theme**:

```dart
dart

ThemeData(
    primaryColor: Colors.blue,
    accentColor: Colors.green,
    buttonTheme: ButtonThemeData(
      buttonColor: Colors.blue, // Sets the
button's background color
    ),
    textTheme: TextTheme(
      headline1:    TextStyle(fontSize:    32,
fontWeight: FontWeight.bold),
      bodyText1:    TextStyle(fontSize:    18,
color: Colors.black),
    ),
```

```
);
```

In this example:

- **primaryColor**: Sets the primary color for the app (used in AppBar, floating action button, etc.).
- **accentColor**: Defines the accent color used for highlighting elements.
- **buttonTheme**: Customizes the button appearance globally.
- **textTheme**: Customizes the text styles used throughout the app.

To apply this theme globally:

dart

```
MaterialApp(
  theme: ThemeData(
    primaryColor: Colors.blue,
    accentColor: Colors.green,
  ),
  home: HomeScreen(),
);
```

Styling Apps for a Polished Look

The appearance and style of your app play a significant role in user experience. By customizing the UI elements, using consistent colors, fonts, and themes, you can create a polished, cohesive app that is visually appealing.

---

1. Consistent Use of Color

Color is one of the most important aspects of UI design. Flutter allows you to easily define your color scheme using `Color` constants, `MaterialColor`, and `ThemeData`.

- **Defining Colors**:

  dart

  ```
  final      Color      primaryColor      =
  Color(0xFF42A5F5); // Custom blue color
  final      Color      accentColor      =
  Colors.orangeAccent; // Predefined color
  ```

- **Using Colors in Widgets**:

  dart

  ```
  Container(
  ```

```
color: primaryColor,
child:    Text('Styled    Text',    style:
TextStyle(color: accentColor)),
);
```

2. Polishing the UI with Padding and Margin

Use padding and margin to create appropriate spacing between elements, which is crucial for readability and a clean layout.

- **Example of Padding and Margin**:

```dart

Padding(
  padding: EdgeInsets.all(16.0),
  child: Container(
    margin: EdgeInsets.symmetric(vertical:
10),
    color: Colors.blue,
    height: 100,
  ),
);
```

3. Responsive Layouts

Ensure that your app looks good on different screen sizes and orientations by using responsive layouts. Widgets like MediaQuery, LayoutBuilder, and Flexible can help you create layouts that adjust to the screen size.

191

- **Example of Responsive Layout**:

dart

```dart
LayoutBuilder(
  builder: (context, constraints) {
    if (constraints.maxWidth > 600) {
      return Row(
        children: [
          Expanded(child: Container(color:
Colors.blue)),
          Expanded(child: Container(color:
Colors.green)),
        ],
      );
    } else {
      return Column(
        children: [
          Container(color:    Colors.blue,
height: 100),
          Container(color:    Colors.green,
height: 100),
        ],
      );
    }
  },
);
```

This layout adapts based on the screen width, displaying widgets in a row on larger screens and a column on smaller screens.

Conclusion

Customizing UI elements in Flutter allows you to create visually appealing, user-friendly apps. By understanding how to style buttons, text fields, cards, fonts, and themes, you can achieve a polished, cohesive look across your app. Additionally, using consistent colors, margins, and padding ensures a well-structured and intuitive UI.

Flutter's flexibility allows you to create custom widgets and styles easily, making it an excellent framework for building beautifully designed apps. Whether you're customizing individual elements or defining global themes, Flutter provides the tools you need to create stunning UIs.

CHAPTER 16

BUILDING A WEATHER APP

Introduction

In this chapter, we will build a simple **Weather App** using Flutter. The app will fetch weather data from an external API and display it dynamically on the screen. We'll also cover handling errors and displaying loading states to improve the user experience.

Fetching Data from a Weather API

To start, we need to fetch weather data from a weather API. For this example, we will use the free and popular **OpenWeatherMap API**. Before proceeding, you'll need to create an account and get an API key from OpenWeatherMap.

1. Setting Up the Project

1. Create a new Flutter project.
2. Add the `http` package to your `pubspec.yaml` file to make HTTP requests.

```yaml
dependencies:
  flutter:
    sdk: flutter
  http: ^0.13.3
```

3. Run `flutter pub get` to install the dependencies.

---

2. Fetching Weather Data

We'll use the `http` package to send a GET request to the OpenWeatherMap API and retrieve the current weather data.

First, create a `WeatherService` class to handle the API call:

```dart
import 'dart:convert';
import 'package:http/http.dart' as http;

class WeatherService {
  final String apiKey = 'YOUR_API_KEY'; // Replace with your API key

  Future<Map<String, dynamic>> fetchWeather(String city) async {
```

```
    final                    url                    =
Uri.parse('https://api.openweathermap.org/data/
2.5/weather?q=$city&appid=$apiKey&units=metric'
);

    final response = await http.get(url);

    if (response.statusCode == 200) {
        return    json.decode(response.body);    //
Parse JSON data
    } else {
        throw  Exception('Failed  to  load  weather
data');
    }
  }
}
```

- **API URL**: The URL is constructed dynamically based on the `city` input and the API key.
- **Fetching data**: The `http.get` method sends a GET request to the API and retrieves the data.
- **Parsing data**: The response body is parsed from JSON into a Dart object (a `Map<String, dynamic>`).

---

3. Handling API Data in the UI

Now let's create the UI to display the weather data. We'll use a `StatefulWidget` to handle dynamic content and fetch data asynchronously.

dart

```dart
import 'package:flutter/material.dart';
import 'weather_service.dart';

void main() {
  runApp(MyApp());
}

class MyApp extends StatelessWidget {
  @override
  Widget build(BuildContext context) {
    return MaterialApp(
      title: 'Weather App',
      theme: ThemeData(
        primarySwatch: Colors.blue,
      ),
      home: WeatherScreen(),
    );
  }
}

class WeatherScreen extends StatefulWidget {
  @override
```

```dart
  _WeatherScreenState     createState()     =>
_WeatherScreenState();
}


class      _WeatherScreenState      extends
State<WeatherScreen> {
  final    WeatherService   _weatherService   =
WeatherService();
  String _city = 'London'; // Default city
  bool _isLoading = false;
  String _errorMessage = '';
  Map<String, dynamic>? _weatherData;

  @override
  void initState() {
    super.initState();
    _fetchWeather();
  }

  // Fetch weather data
  Future<void> _fetchWeather() async {
    setState(() {
      _isLoading = true;
      _errorMessage = '';
    });

    try {
      final     weather     =     await
_weatherService.fetchWeather(_city);
```

```
    setState(() {
      _isLoading = false;
      _weatherData = weather;
    });
  } catch (e) {
    setState(() {
      _isLoading = false;
      _errorMessage = 'Failed to fetch weather
data';
    });
  }
}


// UI to display weather data
@override
Widget build(BuildContext context) {
  return Scaffold(
    appBar: AppBar(
      title: Text('Weather App'),
    ),
    body: Padding(
      padding: const EdgeInsets.all(16.0),
      child: Column(
        crossAxisAlignment:
CrossAxisAlignment.center,
        children: [
          // City input field
          TextField(
```

199

```dart
              decoration:
InputDecoration(labelText: 'Enter city'),
              onChanged: (text) {
                setState(() {
                  _city = text;
                });
              },
              onSubmitted: (_) {
                _fetchWeather();
              },
            ),
            SizedBox(height: 20),

            // Show loading state
            if (_isLoading)
              Center(child:
CircularProgressIndicator()),

            // Show error message
            if (_errorMessage.isNotEmpty)
              Text(
                _errorMessage,
                style:            TextStyle(color:
Colors.red),
              ),

            // Show weather data
            if    (_weatherData    !=    null    &&
!_isLoading)
```

```
Column(
  children: [
    Text(
      'Weather in $_city',
      style:    TextStyle(fontSize:
24, fontWeight: FontWeight.bold),
    ),
    SizedBox(height: 10),
    Text(
      'Temperature:
${_weatherData!['main']['temp']}°C',
        style:    TextStyle(fontSize:
18),
    ),
    Text(
      'Weather:
${_weatherData!['weather'][0]['description']}',
        style:    TextStyle(fontSize:
18),
    ),
    SizedBox(height: 20),
    Image.network(

'https://openweathermap.org/img/wn/${_weatherData!['weather'][0]['icon']}@2x.png',
      height: 100,
    ),
  ],
),
```

```
            ],
          ),
        ),
      );
    }
  }
```

- **State Management**:
  - o `_isLoading`: Boolean to check if the data is being fetched.
  - o `_errorMessage`: String to display any error message.
  - o `_weatherData`: Stores the weather data fetched from the API.

Displaying Dynamic Content Using Flutter's Widgets

In this example, we use several Flutter widgets to display the weather data dynamically:

- `TextField`: Allows the user to enter the name of the city.
- `CircularProgressIndicator`: Displays a loading spinner while data is being fetched.
- `Text`: Displays weather information like temperature and description.
- `Image.network`: Displays the weather icon fetched from the API.

Handling Errors and Loading States

Handling errors and displaying loading states are essential for a smooth user experience. We've implemented error handling using `try-catch` to catch any errors during the API request. If an error occurs, we display an error message in the UI.

- **Loading state**: While the data is being fetched, a loading spinner is shown.
- **Error handling**: If the API request fails, we show an error message like "Failed to fetch weather data".
- **Empty state**: If the weather data is successfully fetched, it is displayed dynamically on the screen.

Conclusion

In this chapter, we've built a **Weather App** that:

1. Fetches weather data from the OpenWeatherMap API using HTTP requests.
2. Displays the weather data dynamically in the UI using Flutter widgets.
3. Handles errors and loading states to ensure a smooth user experience.

With this foundation, you can easily expand the app to include additional features, such as displaying a 7-day forecast, showing weather for multiple cities, or adding more interactive elements. You've learned how to fetch and parse JSON data, handle user input, and display dynamic content in Flutter.

CHAPTER 17

BUILDING A CHAT APPLICATION

Introduction

In this chapter, we will build a **Chat Application** using **Firebase** for real-time communication. Firebase provides a suite of backend services, including authentication, real-time databases, and cloud messaging, which makes it an ideal choice for building a chat app.

The main features we'll cover in this chapter include:

1. **Real-time communication with Firebase** using Firebase Firestore.
2. **Implementing a chat interface** with message input, displaying messages, and handling interactions.
3. **Handling user authentication** using Firebase Authentication, enabling users to sign in and sign out.

By the end of this chapter, you'll have a fully functional real-time chat app where users can sign in, send messages, and interact in real-time.

1. Setting Up Firebase

Before we start coding, we need to set up Firebase for our Flutter app.

1. **Create a Firebase Project**:
    o   Go to the Firebase Console.
    o   Create a new project or select an existing one.
2. **Add Firebase to Your Flutter Project**:
    o   For Android: Follow the instructions to add Firebase to your Android project from the Firebase console (download `google-services.json` and place it in the `android/app` folder).
    o   For iOS: Follow the instructions to add Firebase to your iOS project (download `GoogleService-Info.plist` and add it to the `ios/Runner` folder).
    o   Add the necessary dependencies in your `pubspec.yaml` file:

yaml

```
dependencies:
  flutter:
    sdk: flutter
  firebase_core: ^1.10.6
  firebase_auth: ^3.3.4
```

```
cloud_firestore: ^3.1.5
```

3. **Initialize Firebase**: In your `main.dart`, initialize Firebase before running the app.

```dart
import
'package:firebase_core/firebase_core.dart
';
import 'package:flutter/material.dart';

void main() async {

WidgetsFlutterBinding.ensureInitialized()
;
  await Firebase.initializeApp();
  runApp(MyApp());
}

class MyApp extends StatelessWidget {
  @override
  Widget build(BuildContext context) {
    return MaterialApp(
      title: 'Flutter Chat App',
      theme: ThemeData(
        primarySwatch: Colors.blue,
        visualDensity:
VisualDensity.adaptivePlatformDensity,
      ),
```

207

```
        home: ChatScreen(),
    );
  }
}
```

---

2. Real-time Communication with Firebase

Firebase Firestore is a flexible, scalable NoSQL cloud database used for storing and syncing data in real-time. It provides a way to store and retrieve data easily, which makes it an excellent choice for a real-time chat application.

---

1. Setting Up Firestore

To store messages and retrieve them in real-time, we will use Firestore. Here's how we can set up and store chat messages.

- **Storing Messages in Firestore**:

We will store each message as a document in a `messages` collection in Firestore. Each message will contain fields such as the message content, the sender's user ID, and a timestamp.

dart

```dart
import
'package:cloud_firestore/cloud_firestore.dart';

class ChatService {
  final        FirebaseFirestore        _db        =
FirebaseFirestore.instance;

  // Send a message to Firestore
  Future<void>      sendMessage(String      message,
String userId) async {
    await _db.collection('messages').add({
      'text': message,
      'senderId': userId,
      'timestamp': FieldValue.serverTimestamp(),
    });
  }

  // Get real-time messages
  Stream<List<Message>> getMessages() {
    return _db
        .collection('messages')
        .orderBy('timestamp', descending: true)
        .snapshots()
        .map((snapshot) => snapshot.docs
            .map((doc)                          =>
Message.fromFirestore(doc.data()))
            .toList());
  }
}
```

```
class Message {
  final String text;
  final String senderId;
  final Timestamp timestamp;

  Message({required     this.text,     required
this.senderId, required this.timestamp});

  factory       Message.fromFirestore(Map<String,
dynamic> data) {
    return Message(
      text: data['text'],
      senderId: data['senderId'],
      timestamp: data['timestamp'],
    );
  }
}
```

- **Explanation**:
    - **sendMessage**: This method adds a new message to the Firestore database. It includes the message text, the sender's ID, and a timestamp.
    - **getMessages**: This method retrieves messages from the Firestore database in real-time. The orderBy('timestamp') ensures that messages are ordered by their timestamp in descending order.

210

2. Displaying Messages in the Chat Interface

Next, we'll create the chat interface, where users can see incoming messages in real-time.

- **ChatScreen**: This widget will display the messages and provide an input field to send new messages.

```dart
import
'package:firebase_auth/firebase_auth.dart';
import 'package:flutter/material.dart';
import 'chat_service.dart';

class ChatScreen extends StatefulWidget {
  @override
  _ChatScreenState          createState()          =>
_ChatScreenState();
}

class _ChatScreenState extends State<ChatScreen>
{
  final          _messageController          =
TextEditingController();
  late ChatService _chatService;
  late User _user;

  @override
```

```
  void initState() {
    super.initState();
    _chatService = ChatService();
    _user = FirebaseAuth.instance.currentUser!;
  }


  // Send a new message
  void _sendMessage() async {
    if (_messageController.text.isNotEmpty) {
      await
_chatService.sendMessage(_messageController.tex
t, _user.uid);
      _messageController.clear();
    }
  }


  @override
  Widget build(BuildContext context) {
    return Scaffold(
      appBar: AppBar(title: Text('Chat')),
      body: Column(
        children: [
          // Chat messages display
          Expanded(
            child: StreamBuilder<List<Message>>(
              stream:
_chatService.getMessages(),
              builder: (context, snapshot) {
```

```
              if (snapshot.connectionState ==
ConnectionState.waiting) {
              return          Center(child:
CircularProgressIndicator());
              }

              if (snapshot.hasError) {
              return          Center(child:
Text('Error: ${snapshot.error}'));
              }

              final messages = snapshot.data
?? [];
              return ListView.builder(
                reverse: true,
                itemCount: messages.length,
                itemBuilder: (context, index)
{
                final         message        =
messages[index];
                  return ListTile(
                    title: Text(message.text),
                    subtitle: Text('Sent by:
${message.senderId}'),
                  );
                },
              );
            },
          ),
```

```
          ),
          // Message input field
          Padding(
            padding: const EdgeInsets.all(8.0),
            child: Row(
              children: [
                Expanded(
                  child: TextField(
                    controller:
_messageController,
                    decoration:
InputDecoration(labelText: 'Enter message'),
                  ),
                ),
                IconButton(
                  icon: Icon(Icons.send),
                  onPressed: _sendMessage,
                ),
              ],
            ),
          ),
        ],
      ),
    );
  }
}
```

- **Explanation**:

- **StreamBuilder**: Listens to real-time updates from Firestore and rebuilds the UI whenever a new message is added.
- **ListView.builder**: Displays the messages in a list.
- **TextField**: Allows the user to input a message.
- **sendMessage**: Sends the message to Firestore.

3. Handling User Authentication

Firebase Authentication allows users to sign in and sign up with different methods such as email/password, Google sign-in, and more. For simplicity, we will implement email/password authentication.

1. Setting Up Firebase Authentication

To handle user authentication, use the firebase_auth package.

- **Sign Up and Sign In Methods**:

```dart

import
'package:firebase_auth/firebase_auth.dart';
```

```dart
class AuthService {
  final          FirebaseAuth        _auth        =
FirebaseAuth.instance;

  // Sign up with email and password
  Future<User?>  signUp(String    email,    String
password) async {
    try {
      final   UserCredential   userCredential   =
await _auth.createUserWithEmailAndPassword(
        email: email,
        password: password,
      );
      return userCredential.user;
    } catch (e) {
      throw Exception('Sign Up Failed');
    }
  }

  // Sign in with email and password
  Future<User?>  signIn(String    email,    String
password) async {
    try {
      final   UserCredential   userCredential   =
await _auth.signInWithEmailAndPassword(
        email: email,
        password: password,
      );
```

```
      return userCredential.user;
    } catch (e) {
      throw Exception('Sign In Failed');
    }
  }


  // Sign out
  Future<void> signOut() async {
    await _auth.signOut();
  }
}
```

2. Implementing Sign Up and Sign In in the UI

Add the sign-up and sign-in functionality to the app, allowing users to log in before accessing the chat screen.

```dart

import
'package:firebase_auth/firebase_auth.dart';
import 'package:flutter/material.dart';
import 'auth_service.dart';

class AuthScreen extends StatefulWidget {
  @override
  _AuthScreenState        createState()        =>
_AuthScreenState();
}
```

217

```dart
class _AuthScreenState extends State<AuthScreen>
{
  final            _emailController        =
TextEditingController();
  final            _passwordController     =
TextEditingController();
  final    AuthService      _authService   =
AuthService();
  bool _isSignUp = true;

  // Switch between Sign In and Sign Up forms
  void _toggleForm() {
    setState(() {
      _isSignUp = !_isSignUp;
    });
  }

  // Handle authentication
  void _authenticate() async {
    try {
      if (_isSignUp) {
        await
_authService.signUp(_emailController.text,
_passwordController.text);
      } else {
        await
_authService.signIn(_emailController.text,
_passwordController.text);
```

```
      }
      Navigator.pushReplacement(
        context,
        MaterialPageRoute(builder: (context) =>
ChatScreen()),
      );
    } catch (e) {

ScaffoldMessenger.of(context).showSnackBar(Snac
kBar(content: Text('Error: $e')));
    }
  }

  @override
  Widget build(BuildContext context) {
    return Scaffold(
      appBar: AppBar(title: Text(_isSignUp ?
'Sign Up' : 'Sign In')),
      body: Padding(
        padding: const EdgeInsets.all(16.0),
        child: Column(
          children: [
            TextField(
              controller: _emailController,
              decoration:
InputDecoration(labelText: 'Email'),
            ),
            TextField(
              controller: _passwordController,
```

```
                decoration:
InputDecoration(labelText: 'Password'),
                obscureText: true,
              ),
              ElevatedButton(
                onPressed: _authenticate,
                child: Text(_isSignUp ? 'Sign Up'
: 'Sign In'),
              ),
              TextButton(
                onPressed: _toggleForm,
                child: Text(_isSignUp ? 'Already
have an account? Sign In' : 'Create an account'),
              ),
            ],
          ),
        ),
      );
  }
}
```

Conclusion

In this chapter, we've built a **Chat Application** using Firebase:

1. **Real-time communication with Firebase**: We used Firestore to store and retrieve messages in real-time.

2. **Implementing a chat interface**: We created a simple chat UI using `StreamBuilder` and `ListView`.

3. **Handling user authentication**: Firebase Authentication was used to sign up and sign in users with email/password.

This chat application is a great starting point for adding more features like user profiles, push notifications, and group chats. You can also expand it with other Firebase services, such as Firebase Cloud Messaging for real-time notifications or Firebase Storage to upload images.

CHAPTER 18

INTEGRATING FIREBASE FOR BACKEND SERVICES

Introduction to Firebase (Authentication, Firestore, and Cloud Functions)

Firebase is a powerful platform provided by Google that helps developers build high-quality apps quickly. It offers a suite of backend services, including authentication, databases, cloud storage, and serverless functions. Firebase simplifies backend integration by providing SDKs for Flutter and other platforms, enabling developers to focus more on the user experience while Firebase takes care of the backend.

In this chapter, we will focus on three core Firebase services:

1. **Firebase Authentication**: Allows users to sign up, sign in, and manage their accounts.
2. **Firestore**: A NoSQL cloud database used for storing and syncing data in real-time.
3. **Cloud Functions**: A serverless framework for running backend code in response to HTTP requests, database changes, and more.

We will learn how to integrate Firebase Authentication, use Firestore to store and retrieve data, and set up Cloud Functions for running server-side logic.

1. Firebase Authentication in Flutter Apps

Firebase Authentication simplifies user authentication by providing several sign-in methods, including email/password, Google sign-in, Facebook login, and more. This section will demonstrate how to integrate Firebase Authentication into your Flutter app.

1.1. Setting Up Firebase Authentication

First, ensure you have added Firebase to your Flutter project by following the setup instructions in the Firebase Flutter documentation.

In your `pubspec.yaml` file, include the `firebase_auth` package:

```yaml
dependencies:
  firebase_auth: ^3.3.4
  firebase_core: ^1.10.6
```

Then, run `flutter pub get` to install the dependencies.

Initialize Firebase in `main.dart`:

```dart
import
'package:firebase_core/firebase_core.dart';
import 'package:flutter/material.dart';

void main() async {
  WidgetsFlutterBinding.ensureInitialized();
  await Firebase.initializeApp();
  runApp(MyApp());
}

class MyApp extends StatelessWidget {
  @override
  Widget build(BuildContext context) {
    return MaterialApp(
      title: 'Firebase Integration',
      home: SignInScreen(),
    );
  }
}
```

1.2. Signing Up and Signing In Users

Firebase Authentication allows users to sign up and sign in with email/password. Here's how to handle user authentication.

- **Sign Up Method**:

dart

```dart
import
'package:firebase_auth/firebase_auth.dart';

class AuthService {
  final        FirebaseAuth      _auth       =
FirebaseAuth.instance;

  Future<User?>  signUp(String  email,  String
password) async {
    try {
      final      userCredential      =      await
_auth.createUserWithEmailAndPassword(
        email: email,
        password: password,
      );
      return userCredential.user;
    } catch (e) {
      throw Exception('Sign up failed');
    }
  }
}
```

- **Sign In Method**:

```dart
dart

class AuthService {
  final FirebaseAuth _auth = FirebaseAuth.instance;

  Future<User?> signIn(String email, String password) async {
    try {
      final userCredential = await _auth.signInWithEmailAndPassword(
        email: email,
        password: password,
      );
      return userCredential.user;
    } catch (e) {
      throw Exception('Sign in failed');
    }
  }

  // Sign Out Method
  Future<void> signOut() async {
    await _auth.signOut();
  }
}
```

In the above code:

- createUserWithEmailAndPassword is used for sign-up.
- signInWithEmailAndPassword is used for sign-in.
- signOut signs the user out.

1.3. Handling Authentication State

You can use a StreamBuilder to listen to the authentication state and navigate users based on their sign-in status.

dart

```
class AuthWrapper extends StatelessWidget {
  @override
  Widget build(BuildContext context) {
    return StreamBuilder<User?>(
      stream:
FirebaseAuth.instance.authStateChanges(),
      builder: (context, snapshot) {
        if      (snapshot.connectionState    ==
ConnectionState.waiting) {
          return CircularProgressIndicator();
        } else if (snapshot.hasData) {
          return ChatScreen();  // Signed-in user
        } else {
          return SignInScreen();  // Signed-out
user
```

```
        }
      },
    );
  }
}
```

Here, `authStateChanges` listens for changes to the authentication state, allowing the app to switch between screens based on whether the user is signed in or not.

---

2. Storing and Retrieving Data from Firestore

Firebase Firestore is a flexible, scalable NoSQL cloud database that lets you store data in documents, which are organized into collections. This makes Firestore ideal for real-time apps like chat applications, to-do lists, and more.

2.1. Setting Up Firestore

Add the `cloud_firestore` package to your `pubspec.yaml`:

```yaml
dependencies:
  cloud_firestore: ^3.1.5
```

Then, run `flutter pub get` to install the dependencies.

2.2. Storing Data in Firestore

Firestore stores data in collections and documents. Each document can contain various fields (such as `String`, `int`, `List`, etc.). Here's an example of storing data to Firestore:

dart

```dart
import
'package:cloud_firestore/cloud_firestore.dart';

class FirestoreService {
  final         FirebaseFirestore      _db        =
FirebaseFirestore.instance;

  Future<void>   addUser(String   userId,   String
name, String email) async {
    try {
      await
_db.collection('users').doc(userId).set({
        'name': name,
        'email': email,
        'createdAt':
FieldValue.serverTimestamp(),
      });
```

```
  } catch (e) {
    throw Exception('Failed to add user');
  }
 }
}
```

- **Explanation**:
  - o We're using set to create or update a document in the users collection.
  - o The document ID is the userId, and the fields are name, email, and a timestamp (createdAt).

2.3. Retrieving Data from Firestore

To retrieve data, you can use get to fetch a single document or snapshots for real-time data updates.

- **Fetching a Single Document**:

dart

```
Future<DocumentSnapshot> getUser(String userId)
async {
  try {
    return                                await
_db.collection('users').doc(userId).get();
  } catch (e) {
```

```
    throw Exception('Failed to fetch user');
  }
}
```

- **Real-time Updates**:

dart

```
Stream<List<User>> getUsers() {
  return
_db.collection('users').snapshots().map((queryS
napshot) {
    return querySnapshot.docs
        .map((doc)                              =>
User.fromFirestore(doc.data()))
        .toList();
  });
}
```

- **Explanation**:
    - o snapshots() listens for real-time changes to
      the users collection. Whenever data changes,
      the UI is automatically updated.
    - o map is used to convert Firestore documents into
      custom User objects.

2.4. Example of Fetching and Displaying Users in a List

231

To display a list of users from Firestore, use a `StreamBuilder` to listen for changes:

dart

```dart
class UsersList extends StatelessWidget {
  final FirestoreService _firestoreService =
FirestoreService();

  @override
  Widget build(BuildContext context) {
    return StreamBuilder<List<User>>(
      stream: _firestoreService.getUsers(),
      builder: (context, snapshot) {
        if      (snapshot.connectionState     ==
ConnectionState.waiting) {
          return                    Center(child:
CircularProgressIndicator());
        } else if (snapshot.hasError) {
          return    Center(child:    Text('Error:
${snapshot.error}'));
        } else if (!snapshot.hasData) {
          return  Center(child:  Text('No  users
found.'));
        } else {
          final users = snapshot.data!;
          return ListView.builder(
            itemCount: users.length,
            itemBuilder: (context, index) {
```

```
        return ListTile(
          title: Text(users[index].name),
          subtitle:
Text(users[index].email),
          );
        },
      );
    }
  },
  );
  }
}
```

- **Explanation**:
  - o The `StreamBuilder` listens to the real-time updates from Firestore and rebuilds the widget when the data changes.
  - o The `ListView.builder` is used to display the list of users.

---

3. Firebase Cloud Functions

Cloud Functions for Firebase allows you to run server-side logic in response to Firebase events (such as database changes, authentication triggers, or HTTP requests).

3.1. Setting Up Firebase Cloud Functions

To use Firebase Cloud Functions, you first need to set up the Firebase Functions SDK.

1. Install Firebase CLI and initialize Cloud Functions:

    ```bash
    firebase init functions
    ```

2. In your `functions` directory, install the necessary packages:

    ```bash
    cd functions
    npm install
    ```

3.2. Writing Cloud Functions

Here's an example of a simple HTTP function that returns a greeting:

```javascript
const functions = require('firebase-functions');

exports.greetUser                                     =
functions.https.onRequest((req, res) => {
```

234

```
res.send("Hello, Firebase!");
});
```

You can deploy Cloud Functions with the following command:

```
bash

firebase deploy --only functions
```

Conclusion

In this chapter, we learned how to integrate Firebase into a Flutter app to manage authentication, store and retrieve data using Firestore, and set up Cloud Functions for server-side logic. Firebase provides powerful backend services that make it easy to build and scale apps.

We covered:

1. **Firebase Authentication**: How to implement sign-up and sign-in functionality.
2. **Firestore**: How to store, retrieve, and display real-time data.
3. **Cloud Functions**: How to write simple backend functions for server-side operations.

By integrating Firebase, we've built the foundational backend for a modern app with authentication and real-time database capabilities.

CHAPTER 19

PAYMENT INTEGRATION IN FLUTTER

Introduction

In this chapter, we will explore how to integrate payment gateways in a Flutter app to enable users to make secure payments. Payment integration is essential for apps that offer products or services, and Flutter provides robust support for integrating various payment providers, including **Stripe** and **PayPal**.

We will cover the following key topics:

1. **Integrating Payment Gateways**: Implementing payment methods like Stripe and PayPal.
2. **Building a Checkout System**: Designing the user interface and process for payments.
3. **Handling Transactions Securely**: Best practices for ensuring payment data is handled securely.

1. Integrating Payment Gateways (Stripe, PayPal)

There are various payment gateway providers available, but for this chapter, we will focus on **Stripe** and **PayPal**, two of the most commonly used providers in mobile applications.

1.1. Integrating Stripe in Flutter

Stripe is a powerful payment gateway that supports a wide range of payment methods, including credit cards, debit cards, and wallets. Stripe also offers a Flutter SDK to simplify the integration process.

Step 1: Add Stripe Dependencies

To integrate Stripe in your Flutter project, you need to add the `stripe_payment` or `flutter_stripe` package to your `pubspec.yaml`.

yaml

```
dependencies:
  flutter:
    sdk: flutter
  flutter_stripe: ^4.0.0
```

Then run `flutter pub get` to install the dependencies.

238

Step 2: Initialize Stripe

Before you can use Stripe in your Flutter app, you must initialize it with your Stripe public key. You can find this key in your Stripe dashboard.

```dart
import
'package:flutter_stripe/flutter_stripe.dart';

void main() {
  WidgetsFlutterBinding.ensureInitialized();
  Stripe.publishableKey = 'your-publishable-key-here';
  runApp(MyApp());
}
```

Step 3: Create a Payment Method

To process a payment, you first need to create a payment method (such as a credit card). You can use Stripe's `PaymentMethod` class to do this.

```dart
Future<void> createPaymentMethod() async {
  try {
```

```
    final        paymentMethod      =        await
Stripe.instance.createPaymentMethod(
      PaymentMethodParams.card(
        paymentMethodData: PaymentMethodData(
          billingDetails:   BillingDetails(name:
'John Doe'),
        ),
      ),
    );

    print('Payment       Method        created:
${paymentMethod.id}');
  } catch (e) {
    print('Error creating payment method: $e');
  }
}
```

1.2. Implementing Stripe Checkout

Once you've created a payment method, you can send it to your server to create a payment intent. After the server creates the payment intent, you will use the Stripe Flutter SDK to confirm the payment.

Here's a simplified example of how the complete process works:

1.   Create a **payment intent** on your server (with your secret Stripe key).

240

2. Confirm the payment on the client using the `Stripe` Flutter SDK.

Step 4: Create a Payment Intent (Server-side)

Here's an example of a simple payment intent creation in Node.js (on your server):

```javascript
const stripe = require('stripe')('your-secret-key');

app.post('/create-payment-intent', async (req, res) => {
  const paymentIntent = await stripe.paymentIntents.create({
    amount: 1000, // $10.00
    currency: 'usd',
    payment_method: req.body.paymentMethodId,
    confirmation_method: 'manual',
    confirm: true,
  });

  res.send({
    clientSecret: paymentIntent.client_secret,
  });
});
```

Step 5: Confirm Payment on the Client

241

```dart

Future<void> confirmPayment(String clientSecret)
async {
  try {
    final      paymentIntent      =      await
Stripe.instance.confirmPayment(
      clientSecret,
      PaymentMethodParams.card(
        paymentMethodData: PaymentMethodData(
          billingDetails:   BillingDetails(name:
'John Doe'),
        ),
      ),
    );

    if      (paymentIntent.status      ==
PaymentIntentsStatus.Succeeded) {
      print('Payment successful');
    } else {
      print('Payment failed');
    }
  } catch (e) {
    print('Error confirming payment: $e');
  }
}
```

1.3. Integrating PayPal in Flutter

PayPal offers a simple and secure way to process payments, and integrating it with Flutter requires using the PayPal SDK or a third-party package like `flutter_braintree`.

Step 1: Add the `flutter_braintree` Package

```yaml
dependencies:
  flutter:
    sdk: flutter
  flutter_braintree: ^3.0.0
```

Run `flutter pub get` to install the package.

Step 2: Set Up PayPal Integration

First, you need to initialize PayPal through the Braintree SDK and set up your sandbox environment for testing.

```dart
import 'package:flutter_braintree/flutter_braintree.dart';

Future<void> initiatePayPalPayment() async {
  var request = BraintreePayPalRequest(
    amount: '10.00',
    displayName: 'Flutter PayPal Example',
```

243

```
  );

  BraintreePaymentMethodNonce? result =
      await Braintree.requestPaypalNonce(
    'your-client-token-here',
    request,
  );

  if (result != null) {
    print('PayPal nonce: ${result.nonce}');
  } else {
    print('Payment canceled');
  }
}
```

Step 3: Handle PayPal Payments

After the user authorizes the payment via PayPal, you can use the nonce (a one-time-use token) to process the payment on your server. This nonce is passed to your server for further processing.

---

2. Building a Checkout System

A **checkout system** in a Flutter app usually involves three parts:

1. **Product Selection**: Display products and allow users to add them to their cart.

2. **Payment**: Collect payment information and process it securely via a payment gateway like Stripe or PayPal.

3. **Order Confirmation**: Confirm the order, display a success message, and send the details to the backend.

2.1. Creating a Checkout Screen

Here's an example of a basic checkout screen in Flutter:

dart

```
class CheckoutScreen extends StatefulWidget {
  @override
  _CheckoutScreenState    createState()    =>
_CheckoutScreenState();
}

class       _CheckoutScreenState       extends
State<CheckoutScreen> {
  final           _amountController           =
TextEditingController();

  void _startPayment() {
    // Logic to initiate payment (via Stripe or
PayPal)
    print('Payment started');
  }
```

245

```
@override
Widget build(BuildContext context) {
  return Scaffold(
    appBar: AppBar(title: Text('Checkout')),
    body: Padding(
      padding: EdgeInsets.all(16.0),
      child: Column(
        crossAxisAlignment:
CrossAxisAlignment.start,
        children: [
          TextField(
            controller: _amountController,
            decoration:
InputDecoration(labelText: 'Amount'),
            keyboardType:
TextInputType.number,
          ),
          SizedBox(height: 20),
          ElevatedButton(
            onPressed: _startPayment,
            child: Text('Pay Now'),
          ),
        ],
      ),
    ),
  );
}
}
```

In this example:

- The user inputs the amount they wish to pay.
- Clicking the "Pay Now" button triggers the payment process.

---

3. Handling Transactions Securely

When integrating payment gateways like Stripe and PayPal, security is a critical concern. Always ensure that:

1. **Sensitive data is never exposed**: Never store credit card information or other sensitive payment data on the client. Use tokenization (like the `nonce` from PayPal) and never expose your secret keys in the app.
2. **Use HTTPS**: Always use secure HTTPS connections for API calls, especially when dealing with payment information.
3. **Use Backend for Sensitive Operations**: All critical operations (e.g., creating payment intents or handling payments) should be done on the backend, not directly in the client app.

Firebase Cloud Functions can be used to handle payment logic securely on the server side.

Conclusion

In this chapter, we have covered:

1. **Integrating Stripe and PayPal**: How to add payment gateways to your Flutter app using the respective packages.

2. **Building a Checkout System**: How to create a basic checkout flow with Flutter, where users can input payment information and process transactions.

3. **Handling Transactions Securely**: Best practices for ensuring secure payments by never storing sensitive data on the client and using tokenization methods for payment processing.

Payment integration is a crucial feature for any app offering e-commerce or subscription-based services. By following best practices for security and utilizing powerful tools like Stripe and PayPal, you can provide a seamless and secure payment experience to your users.

CHAPTER 20

UNIT AND WIDGET TESTING IN FLUTTER

Introduction

Testing is a crucial part of any software development process, and Flutter provides a robust testing framework to ensure that your app works correctly and efficiently. In this chapter, we will explore two types of testing in Flutter:

1. **Unit Testing**: Testing individual functions, methods, or classes to ensure they produce the expected results.
2. **Widget Testing**: Testing individual widgets or UI components to verify that they function as expected in isolation.

We will cover how to write both types of tests, how to use Flutter's built-in testing framework, and best practices for ensuring the reliability of your Flutter apps.

1. Writing Unit Tests in Flutter

Unit tests focus on testing small, isolated units of functionality in your app, such as a function or a method. The goal of unit testing is to ensure that your individual methods and functions behave as expected.

1.1. Setting Up Unit Testing in Flutter

Before writing tests, you need to add the `test` package to your `pubspec.yaml` file to enable unit testing:

```yaml
dev_dependencies:
  test: ^1.16.0
```

After adding the `test` package, run `flutter pub get` to install the dependencies.

1.2. Writing a Simple Unit Test

Let's write a simple unit test for a method that adds two numbers. Here's an example:

- **Function to Test**:

dart

```dart
int addNumbers(int a, int b) {
  return a + b;
}
```

- **Unit Test**:

Create a new file in the test directory (e.g., test/calculator_test.dart) and write the following test:

dart

```dart
import 'package:test/test.dart';
import 'calculator.dart'; // Import the file where the addNumbers function is located

void main() {
  group('addNumbers', () {
    test('should return the correct sum of two numbers', () {
      expect(addNumbers(2, 3), 5); // Test the expected output for 2 + 3
      expect(addNumbers(-1, 5), 4); // Test the expected output for -1 + 5
      expect(addNumbers(0, 0), 0); // Test the expected output for 0 + 0
    });
```

```
    test('should return negative sum if both
numbers are negative', () {
        expect(addNumbers(-2, -3), -5); // Test the
expected output for -2 + -3
    });
  });
}
```

In this test:

- **group**: Organizes related tests into a group (e.g., testing the `addNumbers` function).
- **test**: Defines an individual test case, where we check if the output of `addNumbers` is as expected.
- **expect**: Compares the function output to the expected result.

1.3. Running Unit Tests

You can run unit tests by using the `flutter test` command in the terminal:

bash

```
flutter test
```

252

This will run all the tests in the `test` directory and output the results in the terminal.

2. Widget Testing for UI Components

Widget testing is used to test individual widgets in isolation. Unlike unit tests, widget tests interact with the Flutter framework and simulate user interactions. These tests help ensure that your UI behaves as expected.

2.1. Setting Up Widget Testing

Widget testing in Flutter uses the `flutter_test` package, which comes bundled with Flutter. You don't need to add any additional dependencies.

Example: Writing a test for a simple widget that displays a `Text` widget:

```dart
import 'package:flutter/material.dart';
import 'package:flutter_test/flutter_test.dart';
import 'package:my_app/main.dart'; // Replace
with your app's main file
```

```
void main() {
  testWidgets('Test Text Widget', (WidgetTester
tester) async {
    // Build the widget tree
    await tester.pumpWidget(MyApp()); // Replace
with the root widget of your app

    // Find the Text widget by its text content
    final    textFinder    =    find.text('Hello,
Flutter!');

    // Verify that the widget exists in the
widget tree
    expect(textFinder, findsOneWidget);
  });
}
```

In this example:

- **testWidgets**: Defines a widget test case.
- **tester.pumpWidget**: Builds the widget tree for testing.
- **find.text**: Searches for a `Text` widget with the specified text content.
- **expect**: Verifies that the widget exists in the widget tree.

2.2. Interacting with Widgets

Widget tests can simulate user interactions like tapping, scrolling, and entering text. Here's an example of testing a button click:

```dart
testWidgets('Button press should update the
text', (WidgetTester tester) async {
  // Build the widget tree
  await tester.pumpWidget(MyApp());

  // Find the button and text widgets
  final buttonFinder =
find.byType(ElevatedButton);
  final textFinder = find.byType(Text);

  // Verify that the initial text is displayed
  expect(textFinder, findsOneWidget);
  expect(find.text('Press me'), findsOneWidget);

  // Simulate a button press
  await tester.tap(buttonFinder);
  await tester.pump(); // Rebuild the widget tree
after the state change

  // Verify that the text has been updated
  expect(find.text('Pressed!'), findsOneWidget);
});
```

In this test:

- **`tester.tap`**: Simulates a tap on a widget.
- **`await tester.pump`**: Rebuilds the widget tree after the state has changed (important after interactions).
- **`find.text`**: Verifies that the updated text appears in the widget tree.

2.3. Running Widget Tests

Widget tests are run using the same `flutter test` command used for unit tests:

```bash

flutter test
```

3. Using Flutter's Testing Framework

Flutter's testing framework is built around the `test` package, and it provides several types of tests:

- **Unit tests**: Test individual methods or functions in isolation.
- **Widget tests**: Test the UI components in isolation.
- **Integration tests**: Test the entire app or a large portion of it by interacting with multiple widgets and APIs.

For integration testing, you can use the `integration_test` package, which allows you to simulate full user flows within the app.

3.1. Integration Testing Setup

To set up integration testing, add the `integration_test` package to your `pubspec.yaml`:

```yaml
yaml

dev_dependencies:
  integration_test:
    sdk: flutter
  flutter_test:
    sdk: flutter
```

Create a test file (e.g., `integration_test/app_test.dart`) and write an integration test:

```dart
dart

import 'package:flutter_test/flutter_test.dart';
import 'package:integration_test/integration_test.dart';
```

```
import 'package:my_app/main.dart'; // Replace
with your app's main file

void main() {

IntegrationTestWidgetsFlutterBinding.ensureInit
ialized();

  testWidgets('Full app test', (tester) async {
    // Launch the app
    await tester.pumpWidget(MyApp());

    // Interact with the app (e.g., tapping
buttons, entering text)
    await
tester.tap(find.byType(ElevatedButton));
    await tester.pump();

    // Verify app behavior (e.g., checking UI
changes, API responses)
    expect(find.text('Pressed!'),
findsOneWidget);
  });
}
```

Run integration tests with:

```
bash
```

```
flutter test integration_test/app_test.dart
```

4. Best Practices for Testing in Flutter

- **Write clear, concise tests**: Each test should focus on a single behavior and be easy to understand.
- **Test edge cases**: Consider possible edge cases, such as empty input, invalid data, and boundary conditions.
- **Mock dependencies**: Use mocking to isolate the component being tested and avoid dependencies on external resources (e.g., APIs or databases). The `mockito` package is commonly used for mocking in Flutter.
- **Automate tests**: Integrate your tests into your continuous integration (CI) pipeline to run them automatically on every code change.

Conclusion

In this chapter, we've learned the fundamentals of **unit testing** and **widget testing** in Flutter. We explored how to:

1. **Write unit tests** to test individual functions or methods.
2. **Write widget tests** to test UI components and simulate user interactions.
3. Use **Flutter's testing framework** to run both types of tests and ensure that your app functions as expected.

By writing and running these tests, you can identify bugs early, improve the reliability of your app, and ensure that it continues to work correctly as you add new features.

CHAPTER 21

DEBUGGING FLUTTER APPS

Introduction

Debugging is a critical part of the development process that helps you identify and fix issues in your Flutter app. Flutter offers powerful tools to help developers troubleshoot problems efficiently, ranging from simple print statements to advanced profiling tools. In this chapter, we'll cover the most common **debugging techniques**, how to use **Flutter DevTools** effectively, and how to profile app performance to ensure your app runs smoothly.

1. Common Flutter Debugging Techniques

Debugging in Flutter can be done using a variety of techniques, including:

- **Using the Debug Console**
- **Print Statements**
- **Error and Stack Traces**
- **Flutter's Debugging Widgets**

Let's explore these techniques.

1.1. Using the Debug Console

The **debug console** is a simple but powerful tool for viewing logs and error messages. By printing information to the console, you can track variables, view function execution, and understand what's going wrong in your app.

- **Basic Debugging with `print()`**: In Flutter, you can use `print()` to display messages in the console. This is useful for tracing program flow or displaying the value of variables at specific points in your app.

  dart

  ```dart
  print("User input: $userInput");
  ```

- **Log Levels**: You can also use different log levels for better control over logging:

  dart

  ```dart
  debugPrint("This is a debug message");
  ```

`debugPrint` provides better performance than `print()` because it has throttling built in, ensuring you don't flood the console with too many logs.

1.2. Breakpoints and Step-by-Step Debugging

You can set breakpoints in your IDE (such as VS Code or Android Studio) to pause execution at specific points in the code. This allows you to inspect the app's state at that moment and step through the code line by line.

- **Setting Breakpoints**: In your IDE, click on the left margin next to a line of code where you want to pause execution. When the breakpoint is hit, you can inspect variables, call stack, and more.
- **Step Through Code**: Use the step buttons (Step Over, Step Into) to move through the code and evaluate how the app's state changes at each step.

1.3. Error and Stack Traces

When an error occurs, Flutter provides detailed error messages and stack traces that can help you identify and fix issues.

- **Flutter Error Messages**: Flutter errors are typically displayed in the console with useful messages explaining what went wrong. This includes information about the type of error (e.g., `StateError`, `NullPointerException`), along with a stack trace showing where the error occurred in the code.

- **Example of an Error in Flutter**:

```dart
void main() {
  runApp(MyApp());
}

class MyApp extends StatelessWidget {
  @override
  Widget build(BuildContext context) {
    return MaterialApp(
      home: Scaffold(
        body: Center(
          child: Text('Hello World'),
        ),
      ),
    );
  }
}
```

If you forget to initialize a required widget or make a type mismatch, the error trace in the console will direct you to the problematic line of code.

- **Using `flutter run` for Debugging**: You can use the `flutter run` command to run your app in debug mode and see the console output.

```bash

flutter run --debug
```

This command provides detailed debug logs, making it easier to identify issues in real-time.

---

2. Using Flutter DevTools

Flutter DevTools is a suite of performance and debugging tools for Flutter. It provides advanced capabilities for inspecting app performance, widget trees, network activity, and more.

2.1. Setting Up Flutter DevTools

To use DevTools, you must first install it. If you've installed the Flutter SDK, you should already have access to DevTools.

1. **Run your app in Debug mode**: Start your app in the terminal using `flutter run` or through your IDE.
2. **Launch DevTools**: If you're using Visual Studio Code, you can launch DevTools by opening the command palette (`Ctrl + Shift + P` or `Cmd + Shift + P`) and typing "Flutter: Open DevTools".

In Android Studio, simply click on the "Flutter Inspector" tab to access DevTools.

2.2. Key Features of Flutter DevTools

- **Widget Inspector**: Lets you inspect the widget tree of your app and see how widgets are laid out. You can view the widget properties, debug UI, and identify layout issues.
  - **Usage**:
    - Launch the **Widget Inspector** from DevTools to view the structure of your app.
    - Click on any widget in the Inspector to highlight it in the app and view its properties.

- **Timeline View**: This shows how long it takes to perform various operations (e.g., UI rendering, network requests, etc.), helping you identify performance bottlenecks.
  - **Usage**:
    - Use the **Timeline View** to track the performance of your app and identify areas that might need optimization.
    - Track frame rendering times and latency for smoother user experience.
- **Memory View**: Displays real-time memory usage and helps you detect memory leaks or excessive memory consumption.
  - **Usage**:
    - Track memory usage in your app and use the **Heap Snapshot** to understand memory allocation.
    - Identify large objects that might cause memory issues.
- **Network View**: Lets you track network requests and responses, making it easier to debug API calls and network interactions.
  - **Usage**:
    - Monitor **HTTP requests**, their statuses, and data payloads in real-time.

- Check if your app is properly handling network responses, and analyze the request latency.

---

3. Profiling App Performance

Profiling helps you monitor and optimize the performance of your Flutter app. Flutter DevTools includes several tools to help you analyze your app's performance and make improvements.

3.1. Profiling CPU Performance

CPU profiling helps you monitor how your app's resources are used over time. By analyzing CPU usage, you can detect performance bottlenecks, excessive CPU consumption, or frame drops.

- **Steps for Profiling CPU Usage**:
    1. Launch the **Timeline View** in DevTools.
    2. Record the app's CPU usage during interaction (e.g., tapping buttons, scrolling).
    3. Analyze the flame chart to identify CPU-heavy operations or long-running tasks.

3.2. Analyzing Frame Rendering and Performance

To ensure your app delivers smooth performance, you need to monitor the **frame rendering times** and ensure that each frame is rendered in under 16ms (60 frames per second).

- **Steps for Profiling Frame Rendering**:
    1. Open the **Performance Tab** in Flutter DevTools.
    2. Record the app's performance while interacting with UI elements.
    3. Look for "janky" frames, which occur when the rendering time exceeds 16ms.
    4. Optimize the code by reducing unnecessary operations or improving how widgets are built.

3.3. Optimizing Memory Usage

Memory profiling helps you track how much memory your app is consuming and detect potential memory leaks.

- **Steps for Profiling Memory Usage**:
    1. Open the **Memory Tab** in DevTools.
    2. Monitor the **memory heap** and watch for any sudden spikes or excessive memory consumption.

3. Use the **Heap Snapshot** to identify objects that are taking up too much memory.

4. If there are any unreferenced objects still occupying memory, consider fixing them (e.g., by using `dispose()` for widgets or services).

3.4. Optimizing App Launch Time

A common performance issue is a long app launch time. You can use **Flutter DevTools** to monitor and optimize the time it takes for your app to start.

- **Steps for Optimizing Launch Time**:
  1. Open the **Timeline Tab** in DevTools.
  2. Record the app launch process to see how long each part of the app takes to load (e.g., widget loading, initialization, etc.).
  3. Identify which operations take the most time, and try to optimize them (e.g., lazy loading or caching).

Conclusion

In this chapter, we covered essential **debugging and performance profiling** techniques in Flutter. We learned how to use:

1. **Basic debugging techniques** like `print()`, breakpoints, and error stack traces.
2. **Flutter DevTools** for advanced debugging and profiling, including the widget inspector, timeline view, memory view, and network view.
3. **Profiling app performance** to ensure smooth rendering, optimal memory usage, and fast app startup.

By utilizing these tools and techniques, you can identify issues early, optimize performance, and build a more reliable and efficient Flutter app.

CHAPTER 22

ENSURING APP PERFORMANCE

Introduction

Performance is a critical aspect of any mobile application, and Flutter provides powerful tools and techniques to ensure your app runs smoothly. Poor app performance, such as slow rendering, unresponsive UI, or lag, can negatively affect user experience. In this chapter, we will focus on strategies for **optimizing rendering and widget tree**, **using const constructors** for performance, and **handling large datasets efficiently**.

These optimization techniques will help you create a smooth, responsive, and high-performing Flutter app.

1. Optimizing Rendering and Widget Tree

In Flutter, the **widget tree** is the foundation of your UI. Every widget in the tree needs to be rendered and updated when the state changes. However, unnecessary rebuilds or inefficient rendering can degrade app performance.

1.1. Minimizing Rebuilds with `const` Widgets

One of the most effective ways to optimize rendering is by minimizing unnecessary widget rebuilds. Flutter uses a **declarative UI model**, meaning that the UI is rebuilt every time the state changes. However, not all widgets need to be rebuilt.

- **Using `const` Constructors**: If the widget's properties don't change, it can be marked as `const`, meaning that Flutter can optimize the widget's rendering and reuse it without needing to rebuild it.

  o **Example of a `const` widget:**

  ```dart
  class MyWidget extends StatelessWidget {
    const MyWidget({Key? key}) : super(key: key);

    @override
    Widget build(BuildContext context) {
      return Text('This widget never changes');
    }
  }
  ```

- **Why Use `const`?**

273

o When you use `const` constructors, Flutter will treat the widget as immutable and can optimize its rendering. This is especially beneficial for widgets like `Text`, `Icon`, and `Container` when their properties don't change.

o **Performance**: Flutter uses less memory and processing power because it doesn't need to rebuild or redraw `const` widgets.

1.2. Using `const` with Widget Trees

Whenever possible, apply the `const` keyword to widgets in your app's widget tree to reduce unnecessary rebuilds. This is particularly useful for static elements like buttons, icons, and labels that don't change over time.

- **Example with `const` widgets in a list:**

dart

```dart
ListView(
  children: const [
    Text('Item 1'),
    Text('Item 2'),
    Text('Item 3'),
  ],
```

```
);
```

Here, since the `Text` widgets never change, marking them as `const` allows Flutter to optimize their rendering.

1.3. Efficient Use of `StatefulWidget`

A common mistake is using `StatefulWidget` when it's unnecessary. `StatefulWidget` rebuilds the entire widget whenever the state changes, which can be costly if used incorrectly.

- **Example of using `StatefulWidget` unnecessarily**:

```dart
class MyList extends StatefulWidget {
  @override
  _MyListState          createState()           =>
_MyListState();
}

class _MyListState extends State<MyList> {
  @override
  Widget build(BuildContext context) {
    return ListView(
      children: [
```

```
        Text('Item 1'),
        Text('Item 2'),
        Text('Item 3'),
      ],
    );
  }
}
```

In this case, StatefulWidget is not necessary because the widget's state does not change. Instead, use a StatelessWidget to avoid unnecessary rebuilds.

- **Efficient Solution**:

dart

```
class MyList extends StatelessWidget {
  @override
  Widget build(BuildContext context) {
    return ListView(
      children: [
        const Text('Item 1'),
        const Text('Item 2'),
        const Text('Item 3'),
      ],
    );
  }
}
```

Using `StatelessWidget` is more efficient when the widget doesn't require state changes.

2. Using `const` Constructors for Performance

Flutter's performance can be significantly improved by using `const` constructors for widgets that do not change. The `const` keyword tells Flutter that the widget's properties will not change, allowing the framework to optimize rendering by avoiding unnecessary rebuilds.

2.1. Benefits of Using `const` Constructors

- **Less Memory Usage**: Flutter stores `const` widgets in a separate memory location and reuses them, reducing memory consumption.
- **Faster Rendering**: Since `const` widgets do not need to be rebuilt, the rendering process becomes faster and more efficient.
- **Improved App Performance**: Reducing unnecessary widget rebuilding leads to smoother UI transitions and faster app performance.

277

2.2. const with Icon and Text Widgets

The Icon and Text widgets are prime candidates for the const constructor since their properties (such as the icon or text) don't change once set.

- **Example of const with Text and Icon:**

  dart

```dart
const Text('Hello, World!', style: TextStyle(fontSize: 24, color: Colors.blue));
const Icon(Icons.home, size: 40, color: Colors.green);
```

Both the Text and Icon widgets are marked const because their content does not change dynamically.

---

3. Handling Large Datasets Efficiently

When working with large datasets, performance can degrade due to excessive widget rebuilding and memory consumption. Flutter provides several strategies for handling large datasets efficiently without compromising performance.

3.1. Using `ListView.builder` for Lazy Loading

Instead of building all items in a large list at once, you can use the `ListView.builder` widget to build only the visible items. This is known as **lazy loading**, and it helps improve performance by only rendering the items that are currently visible on the screen.

- **Example of using `ListView.builder`:**

dart

```
ListView.builder(
    itemCount: largeDataset.length,
    itemBuilder: (context, index) {
      return ListTile(
        title: Text(largeDataset[index]),
      );
    },
);
```

- **Why Use `ListView.builder`:**
  - o `ListView.builder` only creates widgets for the visible list items, saving memory and processing power.
  - o As the user scrolls, new items are created and old ones are discarded, which is much more efficient than rendering all the items at once.

279

3.2. Efficient Scrolling with `GridView.builder`

If you need to display large datasets in a grid, `GridView.builder` is the most efficient option. It works similarly to `ListView.builder`, but for grids.

- **Example of using `GridView.builder`:**

dart

```dart
GridView.builder(
  gridDelegate:
SliverGridDelegateWithFixedCrossAxisCount
(
    crossAxisCount: 2, // Number of columns
  ),
  itemCount: largeGridDataset.length,
  itemBuilder: (context, index) {
    return Card(
      child: Center(
        child:
Text(largeGridDataset[index]),
      ),
    );
  },
);
```

- **Why Use `GridView.builder`:**

o   `GridView.builder` creates grid items lazily, improving performance when displaying a large number of items.

o   You can define how many items to show per row (using `crossAxisCount`) and manage large datasets in an efficient way.

3.3. Pagination for Large Datasets

When working with very large datasets, consider using **pagination** to load data in chunks. This involves fetching only a subset of data from the server or database at a time.

- **Example of Pagination**:

dart

```
class        PaginatedListView        extends
StatefulWidget {
  @override
  _PaginatedListViewState createState() =>
_PaginatedListViewState();
}

class   _PaginatedListViewState   extends
State<PaginatedListView> {
  List<String> items = [];
```

```dart
int page = 1;
bool isLoading = false;

// Simulate fetching data from the server
Future<void> _fetchData() async {
  if (isLoading) return;

  setState(() {
    isLoading = true;
  });

  // Simulate a network delay
  await Future.delayed(Duration(seconds:
2));

  setState(() {
    items.addAll(List.generate(20,
(index) => 'Item ${index + (page - 1) *
20}'));
    page++;
    isLoading = false;
  });
}

@override
Widget build(BuildContext context) {
  return Scaffold(
    appBar:                     AppBar(title:
Text('Paginated List View')),
```

```
body: ListView.builder(
    itemCount: items.length + 1, // +1
for loading indicator
    itemBuilder: (context, index) {
        if (index == items.length) {
            _fetchData();   // Load next
page of data
            return          Center(child:
CircularProgressIndicator());
        }

        return          ListTile(title:
Text(items[index])));
        },
    ),
);
}
}
```

- **Why Use Pagination**:
    - Pagination reduces the amount of data loaded at any given time, which improves memory usage and app responsiveness.
    - It's particularly useful for apps that need to display large amounts of data retrieved from APIs or databases.

Conclusion

In this chapter, we explored several techniques for optimizing app performance in Flutter:

1. **Optimizing Rendering and Widget Tree**: Minimizing unnecessary rebuilds by using `const` constructors and reducing the use of `StatefulWidget` when not needed.

2. **Using `const` for Performance**: Leveraging `const` constructors to ensure efficient rendering and reduced memory usage.

3. **Handling Large Datasets Efficiently**: Using lazy loading (`ListView.builder` and `GridView.builder`), pagination, and other techniques to manage large datasets without affecting performance.

By applying these techniques, you can significantly improve the performance of your Flutter app, ensuring smooth user experiences even with complex UIs and large datasets.

CHAPTER 23

PREPARING FOR APP DEPLOYMENT

Introduction

Deploying a Flutter app to the Google Play Store and Apple App Store is the final step in the development cycle. However, before you can publish your app, there are several important tasks to handle, such as preparing your app for release, managing permissions and privacy, and building and signing the APK (for Android) or IPA (for iOS) file.

In this chapter, we will walk through the entire deployment process for both **Android** and **iOS**, ensuring your app is ready for distribution to the app stores.

1. Preparing Your App for Release (iOS and Android)

The first step in deploying your app is to prepare it for release. This involves configuring your app for production, removing debug code, and optimizing the app's performance.

1.1. Preparing for Android Release

To prepare your Flutter app for release on Android, follow these steps:

1. **Update App Version**: Ensure that your app's version is set correctly. In `pubspec.yaml`, set the version number and build number.

```yaml
version: 1.0.0+1  # version: 1.0.0, build number: 1
```

2. **Remove Debugging Information**: When you build the app for release, Flutter automatically strips out unnecessary debugging information and optimizes the app's performance. This can be done by running the following command:

```bash
flutter build apk --release
```

3. **Create a Keystore for Signing**: Android requires that all APKs be signed with a key before they can be published. Here's how to create a keystore:

o   Run the following command in your terminal to create a keystore:

```bash
bash
```

```
keytool    -genkey    -v    -keystore
~/.android/key.jks    -keyalg    RSA    -
keysize 2048 -validity 10000 -dname
"CN=your_name, OU=your_organization,
O=your_company,    L=city,    S=state,
C=US"    -storepass    your_password    -
keypass your_key_password
```

o   Place   the   generated   `.jks`   file   in   the `android/app` directory.

4. **Configure the `build.gradle` File**:

o   Open   the   `android/app/build.gradle`   file and   configure   the   signing   settings   under `buildTypes`:

```gradle
gradle
```

```
android {
  buildTypes {
    release {
      signingConfig
signingConfigs.release
    }
  }
```

287

```
}

signingConfigs {
  release {
    storeFile
file("path_to_your_key.jks")
    storePassword "your_password"
    keyAlias "your_key_alias"
    keyPassword "your_key_password"
  }
}
```

5. **Build the APK**: To build a release APK, run:

```bash
bash

flutter build apk --release
```

This generates a release APK in the `build/app/outputs/flutter-apk` directory.

1.2. Preparing for iOS Release

For iOS, the process is slightly different due to the additional requirements of the Apple ecosystem, such as certificates, provisioning profiles, and app signing.

1. **Update App Version**: Similarly to Android, you need to ensure the app's version and build number are updated in `pubspec.yaml`.

2. **Remove Debugging Information**: Flutter removes debug code when you build an app for release. To build the iOS app for release, use:

```bash

flutter build ios --release
```

3. **Set Up App Signing with Xcode**:
   - Open your Flutter project's `ios/Runner.xcworkspace` in **Xcode**.
   - In Xcode, go to **Signing & Capabilities** under the **Runner** target, and ensure that:
     - **Automatically manage signing** is checked.
     - You have selected the correct **team** for app signing (associated with your Apple Developer account).

4. **Create an iOS Distribution Certificate**:
   - Visit the Apple Developer Portal to create an iOS distribution certificate and provisioning profile.
   - Download the certificate and profile and configure them in Xcode.

5. **Build the IPA**: To build the IPA for release, run:

```bash
bash

flutter build ios --release
```

This generates an `.ipa` file in the `build/ios/iphoneos` directory, ready to be distributed.

---

2. Handling Permissions and Privacy

Before you deploy your app, you must manage **permissions** and **privacy** settings. Both iOS and Android require apps to declare permissions for accessing sensitive data like the camera, microphone, location, etc.

2.1. Handling Permissions on Android

In Android, you must request permissions in the `AndroidManifest.xml` file for any resources your app needs to access.

1. **Declare Permissions in the Manifest**: For example, if your app uses location services, add the following to `android/app/src/main/AndroidManifest.xml`:

   ```xml
   xml
   ```

```
<uses-permission
android:name="android.permission.ACCESS_F
INE_LOCATION" />
```

2. **Request Permissions at Runtime**: For Android 6.0 (API level 23) and above, you must request permissions at runtime using the `permission_handler` package.

   o Add the `permission_handler` package to `pubspec.yaml`:

   yaml

   ```
   dependencies:
     permission_handler: ^10.0.0
   ```

   o Request permission in your app:

   dart

   ```
   import
   'package:permission_handler/permiss
   ion_handler.dart';

   void requestPermission() async {
     PermissionStatus status = await
   Permission.location.request();
     if (status.isGranted) {
       // Permission granted
   ```

291

```
    } else {
      // Permission denied
    }
  }
```

2.2. Handling Permissions on iOS

For iOS, you need to specify permissions in the `Info.plist` file, located at `ios/Runner/Info.plist`.

1. **Declare Permissions in `Info.plist`**: For example, to request location permission, add the following to `Info.plist`:

   xml

   ```
   <key>NSLocationWhenInUseUsageDescription<
   /key>
   <string>We need your location to show
   weather information</string>
   ```

2. **Request Permissions at Runtime**: You can use the same `permission_handler` package for runtime permission requests on iOS.

2.3. Privacy Considerations

- **User Data**: Ensure that your app complies with privacy regulations (like GDPR, CCPA). You should explain in your privacy policy how you handle and store user data.
- **App Store Guidelines**: Both the Google Play Store and Apple App Store require apps to include a privacy policy, especially if the app collects sensitive data. Make sure your app complies with these guidelines.

3. Building and Signing the APK/IPA File

Once the app is ready and all configurations are complete, you need to **build and sign** the APK or IPA file to make it ready for distribution.

3.1. Building and Signing the APK (Android)

To generate a signed APK for distribution:

1. Run the following command to build a release version of the APK:

```bash

flutter build apk --release
```

2. The generated APK will be located in `build/app/outputs/flutter-apk/` and can be uploaded to the **Google Play Store**.

3.2. Building and Signing the IPA (iOS)

For iOS, you can either distribute your app via the **App Store** or through **TestFlight** (for beta testing). Here's how to create an IPA file:

1. Ensure you have set up signing in Xcode (as explained above).
2. Open your project in Xcode and select **Generic iOS Device** as the target.
3. In Xcode, go to **Product > Archive** to build the IPA.
4. Once the archive is complete, use the **Xcode Organizer** to export the app and create an IPA file for distribution.

You can then upload the IPA file to **App Store Connect** for submission to the App Store.

Conclusion

In this chapter, we covered the following steps to prepare your app for deployment:

1. **Preparing Your App for Release**: This includes updating version numbers, removing debug code, and configuring signing for both Android and iOS.

2. **Handling Permissions and Privacy**: Properly managing app permissions on both Android and iOS, and ensuring compliance with privacy policies.

3. **Building and Signing APK/IPA Files**: The process of building and signing your Flutter app for release on Google Play and the App Store.

With these steps complete, you are now ready to submit your app to the app stores and share it with users worldwide.

CHAPTER 24

PUBLISHING ON THE GOOGLE PLAY STORE

Introduction

Once your Flutter app is complete, it's time to publish it on the **Google Play Store** to reach your target audience. Publishing an app involves several important steps, from preparing the app for release to managing updates and ensuring that it is discoverable by users. In this chapter, we will guide you through the entire process of publishing your app on the Google Play Store, including app store optimization (ASO) and handling app updates.

1. Step-by-Step Guide to Publishing Your App

Publishing an app on the Google Play Store involves the following steps:

1.1. Set Up a Google Play Developer Account

Before you can publish your app on the Google Play Store, you need to set up a **Google Play Developer account**.

1. Visit the Google Play Console and sign in with your Google account.
2. If you don't have a developer account, sign up for one. The sign-up process involves paying a one-time registration fee of $25 USD.
3. Once registered, you'll have access to the Google Play Console, where you can manage your app, view analytics, and publish new versions.

1.2. Prepare Your App for Release

Once your app is ready, you need to prepare it for release. This involves several steps, such as configuring versioning, signing your app, and building the APK.

- **Update App Version**: Ensure your app version and build numbers are updated in the `pubspec.yaml` file.

```yaml

version: 1.0.0+1
```

- **Sign Your APK**: For Android, you must sign your app before uploading it to the Play Store. This is done using a keystore file, as previously discussed.

- **Build the Release APK**:

Use the following command to build your APK in release mode:

bash

```
flutter build apk --release
```

This will generate the release APK in the `build/app/outputs/flutter-apk/` directory.

- **Create a Keystore (if not already done)**: If you haven't already created a keystore, follow these steps to create one:

bash

```
keytool      -genkey      -v      -keystore
~/.android/key.jks  -keyalg  RSA  -keysize
2048 -validity 10000 -dname "CN=your_name,
OU=your_organization,    O=your_company,
L=city,    S=state,    C=US"    -storepass
your_password -keypass your_key_password
```

1.3. Create a New App Listing on the Google Play Console

1. Log in to the Google Play Console.
2. Click on **"Create App"** to start a new listing for your app.
   - Select the default language (usually English).
   - Enter the app name (this will appear on the Play Store).
   - Choose the app's category (e.g., "Game," "Productivity," etc.).
   - Agree to the developer distribution agreement.

1.4. Upload the APK

After setting up the app listing, you can upload the release APK:

1. Go to the **"Release Management"** section of the Play Console.
2. Select **"App releases"** and choose whether you want to upload a **production**, **beta**, or **alpha** release.
3. Click **"Create Release"**, then **"Browse files"** to select and upload the release APK that was generated in the previous step.
4. Once uploaded, the Play Console will check the APK for any issues (e.g., compatibility with Android versions, required permissions, etc.).

1.5. Add Store Listing Information

In the store listing section, you will need to provide detailed information about your app:

- **App Description**: Provide a short and long description of your app. The short description will appear on the app's listing page, and the long description provides more details about the app's features and functionality.
- **Screenshots**: Upload screenshots of your app in use. These should showcase the key features of the app and be visually appealing. You'll need to upload at least 2-3 screenshots (recommended sizes are 1080x1920 pixels).
- **App Icon**: Upload a high-resolution app icon (512x512 pixels). The icon will represent your app in the Google Play Store.
- **Feature Graphic**: A feature graphic is a banner image that appears at the top of your app's listing on the Play Store. It's optional but recommended for better presentation (recommended size: 1024x500 pixels).
- **Privacy Policy**: If your app collects sensitive user data, you need to provide a privacy policy. This is required by Google Play, and the policy should be hosted on a website.

- **Category and Tags**: Choose a category (e.g., Games, Lifestyle, Education) and provide relevant tags to make it easier for users to find your app.

1.6. Submit for Review

Once you've completed all the required fields, click **"Save"** and **"Review"** to submit your app for review. The Play Store team will review your app to ensure it complies with their guidelines. This process typically takes a few days, but it can take longer depending on the app's complexity.

2. App Store Optimization (ASO)

App Store Optimization (ASO) is the process of improving your app's visibility in the app store and increasing the number of downloads. ASO is similar to SEO (Search Engine Optimization) but focuses on app stores like the Google Play Store.

2.1. Key Elements of ASO

1. **App Title and Short Description**:

- o Choose a descriptive app title with relevant keywords that users are likely to search for.
- o Your short description should clearly describe your app's purpose and include important keywords.

2. **App Icon**:
   - o A clean, visually appealing, and recognizable app icon helps increase click-through rates. Make sure it's easy to identify at a glance and represents the app's functionality.

3. **App Screenshots and Videos**:
   - o High-quality, informative screenshots and videos showcase your app's features. Include captions to highlight key features.

4. **Keywords**:
   - o Use keywords strategically in the app description, title, and tags. Think about what terms potential users might search for to find an app like yours.

5. **App Reviews and Ratings**:
   - o Positive user reviews and ratings increase your app's credibility and rank in the store. Encourage users to leave reviews, but never incentivize them directly.

6. **Regular Updates**:
   - o Regularly updating your app shows users that the app is actively maintained. It also signals to the

Play Store that the app is high-quality and up-to-date.

2.2. Using ASO Tools

There are several tools available to help with ASO, such as:

- **App Annie**: Provides app analytics and helps you track your app's performance, keyword rankings, and competition.
- **Sensor Tower**: Offers keyword research and tracking, competitive analysis, and ASO recommendations.
- **Google Play Console**: Provides data on your app's installs, ratings, and performance, which is valuable for optimizing your ASO strategy.

3. Handling Updates and Versioning

Once your app is live on the Google Play Store, it's important to manage updates and versioning to ensure that users are always using the latest version.

3.1. Versioning and Updating Your App

1. **Version Codes and Version Names**:
   - In Android, every release requires a new **version code** (an integer) and **version name** (a string) that represents the app's version.
   - Update these in the `pubspec.yaml` and `build.gradle` files before building a new release.
   - **Version Code**: Increment the version code for every release. This is used internally by the Play Store.
   - **Version Name**: This is the version string visible to users (e.g., "1.0.1", "2.0.0").

Example in `pubspec.yaml`:

```yaml
```

```
version: 1.0.1+2
```

2. **Building and Publishing Updates**:
   - To submit an update, make changes to your code, increment the version code and version name, and build the new APK or IPA file.
   - Upload the new APK/IPA to the Google Play Console just like you did for the initial release.
   - The Play Store will prompt users to update their app if they have the older version installed.

3.2. Handling Rollbacks and Rejections

- **Rollbacks**: If a new version of the app has issues, you can roll it back by uploading a previous version.
- **Rejections**: If your app is rejected by the Google Play Store team, you'll be notified of the reasons. You'll need to fix the issues and resubmit the app for review.

Conclusion

In this chapter, we've covered the following steps for publishing an app on the **Google Play Store**:

1. **Step-by-Step Guide to Publishing**: How to create a developer account, prepare your app for release, upload the APK, and provide app details.

2. **App Store Optimization (ASO)**: Best practices for improving app visibility and discoverability, including optimizing your title, description, keywords, and screenshots.

3. **Handling Updates and Versioning**: Managing app versioning, handling updates, and ensuring users always have the latest version.

By following these steps, you can successfully publish your Flutter app to the Google Play Store and ensure that it is optimized for discoverability and user engagement.

CHAPTER 25

PUBLISHING ON THE APPLE APP STORE

Introduction

Publishing an app on the **Apple App Store** is an essential step for getting your iOS app in the hands of millions of users. The process involves several steps, including setting up an Apple Developer account, submitting your app for review, and ensuring compliance with Apple's guidelines. In this chapter, we will walk you through the entire process, from setting up your Apple Developer account to submitting your app for review and navigating the App Store guidelines.

1. Setting Up Your Apple Developer Account

Before you can publish an app on the App Store, you need to enroll in the **Apple Developer Program**. This program allows you to submit apps to the App Store and access additional resources and tools for app development.

1.1. Enroll in the Apple Developer Program

1. **Create an Apple ID**: If you don't already have one, create an Apple ID at appleid.apple.com.
2. **Join the Apple Developer Program**:
   - Go to the Apple Developer Program website and sign in with your Apple ID.
   - Click **"Enroll"** to start the registration process.
   - Complete the required information, including your name, address, and contact information.
   - You will be asked to pay the **annual fee of $99 USD** for the Apple Developer Program.
3. **Access Developer Tools**: Once your enrollment is complete, you can access tools such as **Xcode**, **App Store Connect**, and **TestFlight**, which are required for app submission.

1.2. Set Up App Store Connect

App Store Connect is the platform used to manage your apps on the App Store. Here, you can upload your app, manage metadata, view analytics, and track performance.

1. **Sign in to App Store Connect**: Visit App Store Connect and sign in with your Apple ID.
2. **Create Your App's Record**:

- ○ Click **"My Apps"** and then click the "+" button to add a new app.
- ○ Fill in your app's details, including the app name, primary language, bundle ID (which must match the one in Xcode), and the app's SKU (a unique identifier for the app).

2. App Submission Process for iOS

Once your Apple Developer account and App Store Connect are set up, you can start the process of submitting your app. The submission process involves building the app, creating an app listing, and uploading the app for review.

2.1. Prepare Your App for Release

Before submitting your app to the App Store, ensure that your app is prepared for release. This involves:

1. **App Version and Build Number**: In Xcode, update the app version and build number in the **General** tab of your app target.
   - ○ **Version**: This is the version number that users will see (e.g., 1.0.0).

- o **Build**: This is the internal version number for your app (e.g., 1001).

2. **Update App Icons and Screenshots**:
   - o You'll need to upload high-resolution app icons (1024x1024 pixels) and app screenshots for various devices (iPhone, iPad, etc.).
   - o Use **Xcode** to ensure your app icon meets Apple's requirements.

3. **Set Up App Signing and Provisioning**:
   - o Ensure your app is signed correctly using your Apple Developer certificate. In Xcode, go to **Signing & Capabilities** to configure your app's provisioning profile and certificate.

4. **Test Your App**:
   - o Use **TestFlight** to distribute your app to testers and get feedback before submitting it for review. This helps catch any issues and improve the app's quality.

2.2. Create the App Store Listing

In **App Store Connect**, you need to create a detailed listing for your app. This includes metadata, descriptions, screenshots, and other information to help users find and understand your app.

1. **App Name**: Choose a unique and descriptive name for your app.

2. **App Description**: Write a clear, concise description of what your app does. Include any key features and benefits.

3. **Keywords**: Add relevant keywords to help users find your app when they search.

4. **App Category**: Choose the appropriate category for your app (e.g., Games, Lifestyle, Education).

5. **Screenshots and Preview**: Upload screenshots and app previews for various device sizes (iPhone, iPad, Apple Watch). Ensure the screenshots show your app's key features and design.

2.3. Upload the App Using Xcode

1. **Build the IPA File**: In Xcode, select **Generic iOS Device** as the target and then choose **Product > Archive** to build your app.

2. **Upload to App Store Connect**: Once the archive is complete, open **Xcode Organizer** and click **Distribute App**. Follow the steps to upload the app to App Store Connect.

2.4. Submit Your App for Review

311

After uploading the app, you can submit it for review:

1. **Select the Build**: In App Store Connect, go to your app's listing and select the build you just uploaded.
2. **Submit for Review**: Click **"Submit for Review"**. Fill out the required information, including the app's privacy policy, age rating, and any special requirements (such as location access or camera usage).
3. **App Review Process**: The Apple review team will check your app for compliance with their guidelines. The review process usually takes a few days, but it may take longer if there are issues or questions.

---

3. App Store Guidelines and Review Process

Apple has strict guidelines for apps submitted to the App Store. These guidelines cover a wide range of topics, from app functionality and content to user privacy and security.

3.1. App Store Guidelines

Apple's **App Store Review Guidelines** ensure that apps are high-quality, reliable, and meet user expectations. The guidelines include rules on:

1. **App Functionality**: Your app should be fully functional and not contain bugs. It must provide useful and meaningful content to the user.

2. **User Interface**: Apple emphasizes a clean, consistent, and intuitive user interface. Apps that violate Apple's human interface guidelines may be rejected.

3. **Content**: Ensure that your app doesn't include offensive, inappropriate, or harmful content. Apple rejects apps with explicit content or that promote illegal activities.

4. **Privacy**: Your app must respect user privacy, including data collection, sharing, and security. If your app collects personal data, you must provide a privacy policy and obtain user consent.

5. **Monetization**: If your app offers in-app purchases or subscriptions, ensure that you are using the correct in-app purchase APIs.

You can review the full App Store Review Guidelines at Apple's website.

3.2. App Review Process

Apple's app review process involves a thorough inspection of your app to ensure it meets their guidelines. The review team checks for the following:

- **Functionality**: The app should work as expected and meet the functionality described in the app listing.

- **UI Design**: The app's user interface should be intuitive and comply with Apple's design guidelines.

- **Content**: The app should be free of offensive or harmful content.

- **Privacy Compliance**: The app must comply with privacy laws, including the General Data Protection Regulation (GDPR) if applicable.

During the review, the app may be accepted, rejected, or sent back for changes. If rejected, you will receive a detailed explanation of why your app was not accepted.

3.3. Handling Rejections and Resubmissions

If your app is rejected, you can address the issues and resubmit it for review. Common reasons for rejection include:

- **Broken functionality**: The app crashes or doesn't work as expected.

- **Design issues**: The app doesn't meet Apple's UI/UX standards.

- **Privacy concerns**: The app doesn't adequately protect user data or violates privacy laws.

To resubmit, fix the issues, and follow the same steps to upload the updated version of the app.

Conclusion

Publishing an app on the **Apple App Store** involves several steps, including setting up an Apple Developer account, preparing your app for release, creating a detailed app listing, uploading the app, and submitting it for review. Additionally, understanding Apple's **App Store guidelines** and ensuring compliance with them is crucial for successful app submission.

Here's a summary of the steps:

1. **Set up your Apple Developer account** and sign in to App Store Connect.
2. **Prepare your app for release** by updating version numbers, setting up signing, and building the app.
3. **Create a detailed app listing** with a description, screenshots, and other metadata.
4. **Upload your app** using Xcode and submit it for review.
5. **Understand and follow App Store guidelines** to ensure your app is approved.

By following these steps, you can successfully publish your app on the Apple App Store and make it available to millions of iOS users around the world.

CHAPTER 26

INTEGRATING WITH NATIVE CODE

Introduction

One of the strengths of Flutter is its ability to run on multiple platforms, but sometimes you need to write platform-specific code to access native features or APIs. Flutter allows you to integrate with native code through **Platform Channels**, enabling you to communicate with Java, Swift, Kotlin, or Objective-C code. This chapter will cover how to integrate native code with Flutter, how to write platform-specific code, and how to use **Platform Channels** to bridge the gap between Flutter and native APIs.

By the end of this chapter, you will understand how to:

1. **Write custom platform-specific code** in languages like Java, Kotlin, and Swift.
2. **Use Platform Channels** to communicate between Flutter and native code.
3. **Access native libraries and APIs** in your Flutter app.

316

1. Writing Custom Platform-Specific Code (Java, Swift, Kotlin)

When building Flutter apps, you often need to interact with platform-specific APIs that Flutter does not provide out of the box. Flutter supports native development for both Android (Java/Kotlin) and iOS (Objective-C/Swift).

In these cases, you can write **custom platform-specific code** and then call that code from your Flutter app using **Platform Channels**.

1.1. Writing Platform-Specific Code for Android (Java/Kotlin)

Android apps are typically written in Java or Kotlin. If you need to access Android-specific features, you can write code in these languages and call it from Flutter.

1. **Create a MethodChannel in Flutter**:

   In your Flutter app, define a **MethodChannel** to communicate with the native Android code.

   dart

   ```
   import 'package:flutter/services.dart';
   ```

```
class NativeBridge {
  static const MethodChannel _channel =
MethodChannel('com.example/native');

  // Method to call native Android code
  Future<String> getBatteryLevel() async {
    try {
      final String batteryLevel = await
_channel.invokeMethod('getBatteryLevel');
      return batteryLevel;
    } on PlatformException catch (e) {
      return "Failed to get battery level:
'${e.message}'.";
    }
  }
}
```

2. **Implement the Native Code in Android (Java/Kotlin)**:

In your Android project (inside the `android/` directory), you need to write the native code that will handle the method channel. For example, to get the battery level:

- Open `MainActivity.java` or `MainActivity.kt` inside `android/app/src/main/java/com/example/yourapp/`.
- Add the code to handle the method call in the native Android part of your app:

```java
java

import android.os.Bundle;
import android.os.BatteryManager;
import io.flutter.app.FlutterActivity;
import
io.flutter.plugin.common.MethodChannel;

public class MainActivity extends
FlutterActivity {
    private static final String CHANNEL =
"com.example/native";

    @Override
    public void configureFlutterEngine() {
        super.configureFlutterEngine();

        new
MethodChannel(getFlutterEngine().getDartE
xecutor(), CHANNEL)
                .setMethodCallHandler(
                    (call, result) -> {
                        if
(call.method.equals("getBatteryLevel")) {
                            int
batteryLevel = getBatteryLevel();
                            if
(batteryLevel != -1) {
```

```
result.success("Battery      level:      "     +
batteryLevel + "%");
                              } else {

result.error("UNAVAILABLE", "Battery level
not available.", null);
                    }
              } else {

result.notImplemented();
                         }
                    }
              );
    }

    private int getBatteryLevel() {
        BatteryManager   batteryManager   =
(BatteryManager)
getSystemService(BATTERY_SERVICE);
        return
batteryManager.getIntProperty(BatteryMana
ger.BATTERY_PROPERTY_CAPACITY);
    }
}
```

3. **Call the Native Code from Flutter**: When the getBatteryLevel() method is called in Flutter, it

sends a message to the native Android code, which processes it and returns the battery level.

1.2. Writing Platform-Specific Code for iOS (Swift/Objective-C)

For iOS, you can use Swift or Objective-C to write native code. Below is an example of how to implement platform-specific code using Swift.

1. **Create a MethodChannel in Flutter**:

     As with Android, define a **MethodChannel** in Flutter:

     dart

```
class NativeBridge {
  static const MethodChannel _channel =
MethodChannel('com.example/native');

  Future<String> getBatteryLevel() async {
    try {
      final String batteryLevel = await
_channel.invokeMethod('getBatteryLevel');
      return batteryLevel;
    } on PlatformException catch (e) {
```

```
        return "Failed to get battery level:
'${e.message}'.";
    }
  }
}
```

2. **Implement the Native Code in iOS (Swift)**:

   o Open the `AppDelegate.swift` file in the `ios/Runner/` directory.

   o Add the following code to handle the method channel:

```swift
import UIKit
import Flutter
import CoreBattery

@UIApplicationMain
@objc class AppDelegate:
FlutterAppDelegate {
    private let channelName =
"com.example/native"

    override func application(
        _ application: UIApplication,
        didFinishLaunchingWithOptions
launchOptions:
[UIApplication.LaunchOptionsKey: Any]?
```

322

```swift
) -> Bool {
    let            controller        :
FlutterViewController                 =
window?.rootViewController           as!
FlutterViewController
        let        batteryChannel     =
FlutterMethodChannel(name: channelName,

binaryMessenger:
controller.binaryMessenger)


batteryChannel.setMethodCallHandler     {
(call:      FlutterMethodCall,       result:
@escaping FlutterResult) in
            if        call.method       ==
"getBatteryLevel" {

self.getBatteryLevel(result: result)
            } else {

result(FlutterMethodNotImplemented)
            }
        }

        return
super.application(application,
didFinishLaunchingWithOptions:
launchOptions)
```

```
        }

    private  func  getBatteryLevel(result:
FlutterResult) {
        let device = UIDevice.current
        device.isBatteryMonitoringEnabled
= true
        let        batteryLevel        =
device.batteryLevel

        if batteryLevel == -1.0 {
            result(FlutterError(code:
"UNAVAILABLE",

                            message:
"Battery level not available.",

                            details:
nil))
        } else {
            result("Battery        level:
\(batteryLevel * 100)%")
        }
    }
}
```

3. **Call the Native Code from Flutter**: Just like the Android example, when the `getBatteryLevel()` method is invoked in Flutter, it calls the native code, retrieves the battery level, and returns it to Flutter.

2. Platform Channels in Flutter

Platform Channels provide a way to communicate between your Flutter code and the native platform (Android or iOS). You can pass data between Flutter and native code using three main types of platform channels:

1. **Method Channel**: Used to send a message from Flutter to the native code and get a response.
2. **Event Channel**: Used to receive streams of data from the native code (e.g., real-time data or continuous events like sensor data).
3. **Basic Message Channel**: Used for simpler communication that doesn't involve method calls or streams of data.

2.1. Method Channel Example

- **Dart Code**:

```dart
static const MethodChannel _channel =
MethodChannel('com.example/native');
```

325

```
Future<void> getBatteryLevel() async {
  try {
    final int batteryLevel = await
_channel.invokeMethod('getBatteryLevel');
    print("Battery              level:
$batteryLevel%");
  } on PlatformException catch (e) {
    print("Failed to get battery level:
${e.message}");
  }
}
```

- **Native Android (Kotlin/Java)**:

java

```
new
MethodChannel(getFlutterEngine().getDartE
xecutor(), "com.example/native")
    .setMethodCallHandler(
        (call, result) -> {
            if
(call.method.equals("getBatteryLevel")) {
                int      batteryLevel      =
getBatteryLevel();

result.success(batteryLevel);
            } else {
                result.notImplemented();
            }
```

326

```
        }
    );
```

- **Native iOS (Swift)**:

```swift
swift

batteryChannel.setMethodCallHandler        {
(call:        FlutterMethodCall,        result:
@escaping FlutterResult) in
    if call.method == "getBatteryLevel" {
        self.getBatteryLevel(result:
result)
    } else {

result(FlutterMethodNotImplemented)
    }
}
```

2.2. Event Channel Example

Event Channels allow continuous streams of data, such as real-time updates from sensors or audio playback.

- **Dart Code**:

```dart
dart
```

```
static   const   EventChannel   _channel   =
EventChannel('com.example/sensorData');

void startListening() {

_channel.receiveBroadcastStream().listen(
(data) {
    print("Sensor data: $data");
  });
}
```

- **Native Android (Kotlin/Java)**:

```java
new
EventChannel(getFlutterEngine().getDartEx
ecutor(), "com.example/sensorData")
    .setStreamHandler(
        new EventChannel.StreamHandler() {
            @Override
            public   void   onListen(Object
arguments, EventSink events) {
                // Send continuous data
(e.g., sensor data) to Flutter
                events.success("Sensor
data");
            }

            @Override
```

```
            public    void    onCancel(Object
arguments) {
                // Stop sending data when
canceled
            }
        }
    );
```

- **Native iOS (Swift)**:

```swift
eventChannel.setStreamHandler                    {
(arguments, events) in
    // Stream sensor data to Flutter
    events?.success("Sensor data")
}
```

3. Using Native Libraries and APIs in Flutter

Flutter allows you to use **native libraries** and **APIs** that are not available through Flutter's existing plugins. You can achieve this by writing custom platform code and integrating libraries that are already used in native apps.

For example, if you want to use a native Android library (like a third-party SDK for analytics), you would:

1. Add the library to your `android/app/build.gradle` file.
2. Write the integration code in the native Android part of your project (Java/Kotlin).
3. Communicate with that code using **Platform Channels** from Flutter.

Conclusion

In this chapter, we've learned how to:

1. **Write custom platform-specific code** in Java, Kotlin, and Swift.
2. Use **Platform Channels** to communicate between Flutter and native code.
3. **Access native libraries and APIs** in your Flutter app for functionality that isn't provided out of the box by Flutter.

Integrating with native code is powerful for accessing platform-specific features and libraries, and Flutter makes it easy to bridge the gap between the Flutter framework and native Android/iOS code.

CHAPTER 27

FUTURE OF FLUTTER AND MOBILE DEVELOPMENT

Introduction

Flutter has quickly become one of the most popular frameworks for mobile app development, with its unique combination of fast development cycles, a single codebase for multiple platforms, and a robust community. However, as technology continues to evolve, so too does Flutter. In this chapter, we will discuss the **future of Flutter**, **upcoming features**, and the **role of Flutter** in the broader landscape of mobile app development. Additionally, we will explore the **trends in cross-platform development** and how Flutter will continue to shape the future of mobile development.

1. What's Next for Flutter? Updates and Upcoming Features

Flutter has been rapidly evolving since its inception, and its roadmap includes several exciting features that will enhance the framework's capabilities, improve performance, and simplify the development process.

331

1.1. Flutter for Web and Desktop

While Flutter has already made significant strides in mobile app development, **Flutter for Web** and **Flutter for Desktop** are two key areas of future growth.

- **Flutter Web**: Initially in beta, Flutter Web has now become stable, allowing developers to use Flutter to build responsive, high-performance web applications. The primary advantage of using Flutter Web is that you can write one codebase that works across iOS, Android, web browsers, and even desktop.
- **Flutter for Desktop**: With support for macOS, Windows, and Linux, Flutter is making its way to the desktop. While not yet as mature as mobile support, it promises to provide a single codebase for desktop, mobile, and web apps, reducing development time and effort.

Upcoming Improvements:

- o **Performance Enhancements**: Flutter is working on improving rendering performance for web and desktop applications, ensuring that it can handle more complex use cases and provide a smoother experience across different platforms.

o **Tooling and Debugging**: As Flutter Web and Desktop mature, expect significant improvements in tooling, debugging, and IDE integration, making it easier to develop, test, and deploy apps.

1.2. Flutter 3 and Beyond: Improvements and New Features

The Flutter team has been actively working on several key features for future releases of Flutter, including:

- **Null Safety**: Flutter's **null safety** feature, which ensures that variables cannot be null unless explicitly stated, will be continuously improved to make code more reliable and reduce runtime errors.
- **Improved Performance**: Flutter 3 will focus on optimizing app performance by enhancing the framework's engine and reducing app startup time, ensuring even faster app launches and smoother user experiences.
- **State Management Updates**: Flutter has a growing ecosystem of state management libraries, and there is an ongoing effort to improve and standardize state management. The goal is to make it easier for developers

to manage the state of large apps and improve maintainability.

- **Improved Integration with Firebase**: Firebase has become the go-to backend for Flutter apps, and future versions of Flutter will continue to integrate seamlessly with Firebase services, providing even more powerful tools for app development.

1.3. Flutter 3.0 and Dart Enhancements

The **Dart programming language**, which Flutter is built on, is also undergoing improvements that will benefit Flutter developers:

- **Better Concurrency Support**: Dart will continue to improve its concurrency model, making it easier to handle asynchronous operations and manage background tasks.
- **Improvements in Package Ecosystem**: The Dart and Flutter ecosystem will continue to grow, with more packages and plugins being created for common use cases like analytics, authentication, and real-time data synchronization.
- **Dart DevTools Updates**: Dart DevTools will receive updates to provide better insights into performance,

memory usage, and debugging, making the development process more efficient and user-friendly.

2. Cross-Platform Development Trends

As mobile app development has evolved, the demand for **cross-platform frameworks** like Flutter has increased. Here's a look at some of the key trends in cross-platform development:

2.1. The Rise of Cross-Platform Development Frameworks

The concept of **write once, run anywhere** has become a key principle for modern app development. Cross-platform frameworks like **Flutter, React Native, Xamarin**, and **Ionic** enable developers to build apps for multiple platforms using a single codebase. This trend is likely to continue as businesses seek ways to cut down on development time and costs.

- **Flutter vs React Native**: Both Flutter and React Native are dominant players in the cross-platform space. While React Native has been around longer, Flutter has gained significant momentum due to its native performance and comprehensive widget library. Flutter's fast-growing community and ongoing improvements make it a strong contender in the cross-platform development race.

335

- **Unified User Experiences**: Cross-platform frameworks are focusing more on providing **native-like experiences** across multiple platforms. Flutter's UI rendering engine and widget-based architecture ensure that developers can create apps that look and feel native on iOS and Android with minimal effort.

2.2. The Importance of Native Performance

Although cross-platform development is growing, **native performance** remains a priority for many developers. As a result, frameworks like Flutter have made strides in reducing the performance gap between native apps and cross-platform apps.

- **Native-like Performance with Flutter**: Flutter's custom rendering engine allows it to draw its UI elements directly on the canvas, giving it a significant performance advantage over some other cross-platform frameworks. Flutter's **hot reload** and **fast compilation** also help maintain a high development velocity without sacrificing performance.
- **Native Code Integration**: For scenarios where cross-platform frameworks can't fully replicate the functionality of native apps (e.g., using specific hardware features), **platform channels** allow Flutter to call native

APIs and libraries, enabling developers to integrate with platform-specific code when needed.

2.3. Progressive Web Apps (PWAs) and Flutter

Progressive Web Apps (PWAs) are gaining popularity as a lightweight alternative to traditional mobile apps. PWAs combine the best features of native apps and web apps, allowing users to access them via a browser while still offering app-like experiences.

- **Flutter for Web and PWAs**: With Flutter's support for web development, building Progressive Web Apps is becoming easier. Developers can create a Flutter app that works seamlessly on iOS, Android, web, and desktop, all from the same codebase.
- **The Future of PWAs**: As mobile usage continues to rise, PWAs will play a key role in providing users with seamless access to apps without needing to download them from the App Store or Play Store.

3. Flutter's Role in the Future of Mobile App Development

Flutter's **cross-platform nature**, **native performance**, and **rich ecosystem** position it as a key player in the future of mobile app

337

development. Here are some of the ways Flutter is shaping the future of mobile development:

3.1. Flutter as the Future of Mobile Development

- **One Codebase for Multiple Platforms**: With Flutter's growing support for mobile, web, and desktop platforms, the ability to maintain a single codebase for all platforms is becoming more achievable. This will continue to be a major advantage for businesses and developers who need to create apps for multiple platforms quickly and efficiently.

- **Flutter for the Enterprise**: Large enterprises are increasingly adopting Flutter for their mobile and desktop app development. Its fast development cycle, customizability, and growing support from Google make it a powerful tool for enterprise-grade apps.

3.2. Flutter and IoT (Internet of Things)

As the **Internet of Things (IoT)** continues to grow, Flutter will play a key role in developing apps that interact with IoT devices. With its native performance and ability to integrate with native

338

code, Flutter will be a suitable choice for building apps that interact with hardware like sensors, smart devices, and more.

3.3. Integration with Emerging Technologies

- **AI and ML**: As artificial intelligence (AI) and machine learning (ML) become more prevalent in mobile apps, Flutter will continue to integrate with popular AI and ML frameworks like TensorFlow Lite, allowing developers to build smarter apps that use AI to enhance user experiences.
- **AR and VR**: Flutter is also expected to continue evolving to support **augmented reality (AR)** and **virtual reality (VR)** apps. As AR/VR experiences grow, Flutter can leverage platform channels to integrate with native AR/VR libraries, such as Apple's ARKit or Google's ARCore.

Conclusion

In this chapter, we've explored the **future of Flutter** and its role in the rapidly evolving landscape of mobile app development. Key takeaways include:

1. **Flutter's Growth**: Flutter is expanding its reach to web and desktop platforms, making it a true cross-platform framework.

2. **Cross-Platform Trends**: Cross-platform development frameworks like Flutter will continue to grow in popularity as they provide faster, more cost-effective ways to build apps for multiple platforms.

3. **Native Performance and Flexibility**: Flutter's ability to offer near-native performance while maintaining the flexibility of cross-platform development positions it as a leading framework in the mobile development space.

4. **Emerging Technologies**: Flutter will continue to play a role in integrating with emerging technologies like AI, IoT, and AR/VR, further solidifying its position as the future of mobile development.

With **Flutter** evolving rapidly and consistently improving, it's clear that Flutter will be at the forefront of mobile app development for years to come.

www.ingramcontent.com/pod-product-compliance
Lightning Source LLC
LaVergne TN
LVHW051429050326
832903LV00030BD/2999